Bundle Up Baby Quilts

Contents

05 Crazy For Baby
09 Log Cabin Lullaby
15 Baby Bella
21 Sailboat
25 Giggles
29 I Love You This Much
37 All Aboard
41 Playdate
45 Oh Baby
51 The Place You'll Go
56 General Instructions

Crazy For Baby

Your little ray of sunshine will beam at the sight of this citrus-colored quilt! Of course, the design is just as happy when created in blue, green, and purple.

Design by Me & My Sister Designs • Barbara Groves & Mary Jacobson

YARDAGE REQUIREMENTS

Yardage is based on 43"/44" (109 cm/112 cm) wide fabric.

$1^1/_8$ yds (1 m) of orange novelty print fabric

$^5/_8$ yd (57 cm) of white polka-dot fabric

$^1/_4$ yd (23 cm) each of 6 orange print fabrics

$3^3/_8$ yds (3.1 m) of fabric for backing

$^1/_2$ yd (46 cm) of fabric for binding

You will also need:

54" x 60" (137 cm x 152 cm) piece of batting

FINISHED BLOCK SIZE:

6" x 6"
(15 cm x 15 cm)

FINISHED QUILT SIZE:

$45^1/_2$" x $51^1/_2$"
(116 cm x 131 cm)

CUTTING OUT THE PIECES

Follow Rotary Cutting, page 56, to cut fabric.Cut all strips from the selvage-to-selvage width of the fabric.

All measurements include $^1/_4$" seam allowances.

From orange novelty print fabric:

- Cut 1 center rectangle $24^1/_2$" x $30^1/_2$".
- Cut 5 border strips 2"w.

From white polka-dot fabric:

- Cut 5 strips $3^7/_8$"w. From these strips, cut 44 squares $3^7/_8$" x $3^7/_8$".

From each of 4 of the 6 orange print fabrics:

- Cut 1 strip $3^7/_8$"w. From this strip, cut 8 squares $3^7/_8$" x $3^7/_8$".
- Cut 1 strip $3^1/_2$"w. From this strip, cut 6 rectangles $3^1/_2$" x $5^1/_2$".

From each of the 2 remaining orange print fabrics:

- Cut 1 strip $3^7/_8$"w. From this strip, cut 6 squares $3^7/_8$" x $3^7/_8$".
- Cut 1 strip $3^1/_2$"w. From this strip, cut 6 rectangles $3^1/_2$" x $5^1/_2$".

From fabric for binding:

- Cut 6 strips $2^1/_4$"w.

MAKING THE BLOCKS

Follow Piecing, page 57, and Pressing, page 57, to make Blocks. Use $^1/_4$" seam allowances throughout.

1. Draw diagonal line (corner to corner) on wrong side of each white polka-dot square. With right sides together, place 1 white polka-dot square on top of 1 orange print square. Stitch seam $^1/_4$" from each side of drawn line (Fig. 1).

Fig. 1

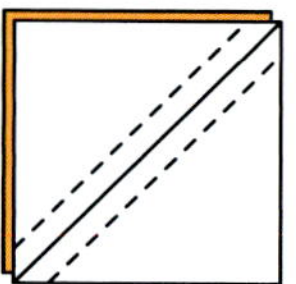

2. Cut along drawn line and press seam allowance to darker fabric to make 2 Triangle-Squares. Make 88 Triangle-Squares.

Triangle-Squares
(make 88)

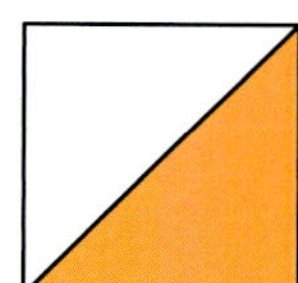

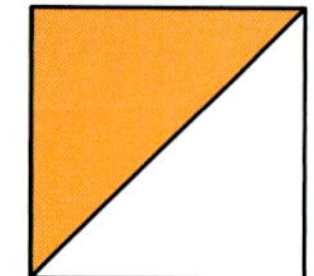

3. Sew 4 matching Triangle-Squares together to make Block. Make 22 Blocks.

Block (make 22)

ASSEMBLING THE QUILT TOP CENTER

1. Sew 5 Blocks together to make Unit 1. Make 2 Unit 1's.

Unit 1
(make 2)

2. Sew 6 Blocks together to make Unit 2. Make 2 Unit 2's.

Unit 2
(make 2)

3. Referring to Quilt Top Diagram, sew 1 Unit 1 to each side of center rectangle, and then sew 1 Unit 2 to top and bottom to complete quilt top center.

Quilt Top Diagram

ADDING THE BORDERS

1. Sew border strips together, end to end, to make 1 continuous inner border strip.
2. To determine length of side inner borders, measure length across center of quilt top center. Cut 2 side inner borders the determined length from inner border strip. Matching centers and corners, sew side inner borders to quilt top center.
3. To determine length of top/bottom inner borders, measure width across center of quilt top (including added borders). Cut 2 top/bottom inner borders the determined length from inner border strip. Matching centers and corners, sew top/bottom inner borders to quilt top.
4. Sew 9 rectangles together to make outer border. Make 4 outer borders.

Outer Border
(make 4)

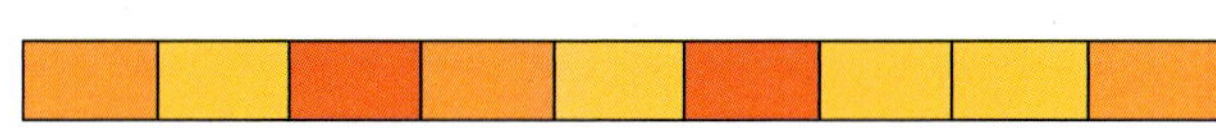

5. Matching centers and corners and easing any fullness, sew side, top, and then bottom outer borders to quilt top.

COMPLETING THE QUILT

1. Follow Quilting, page 60, to mark, layer, and quilt as desired. Our quilt is machine quilted in a loop pattern.
2. Follow Making a Hanging Sleeve, page 64, if a hanging sleeve is desired.
3. Follow Binding, page 65, to make and then attach straight-grain binding with mitered corners.

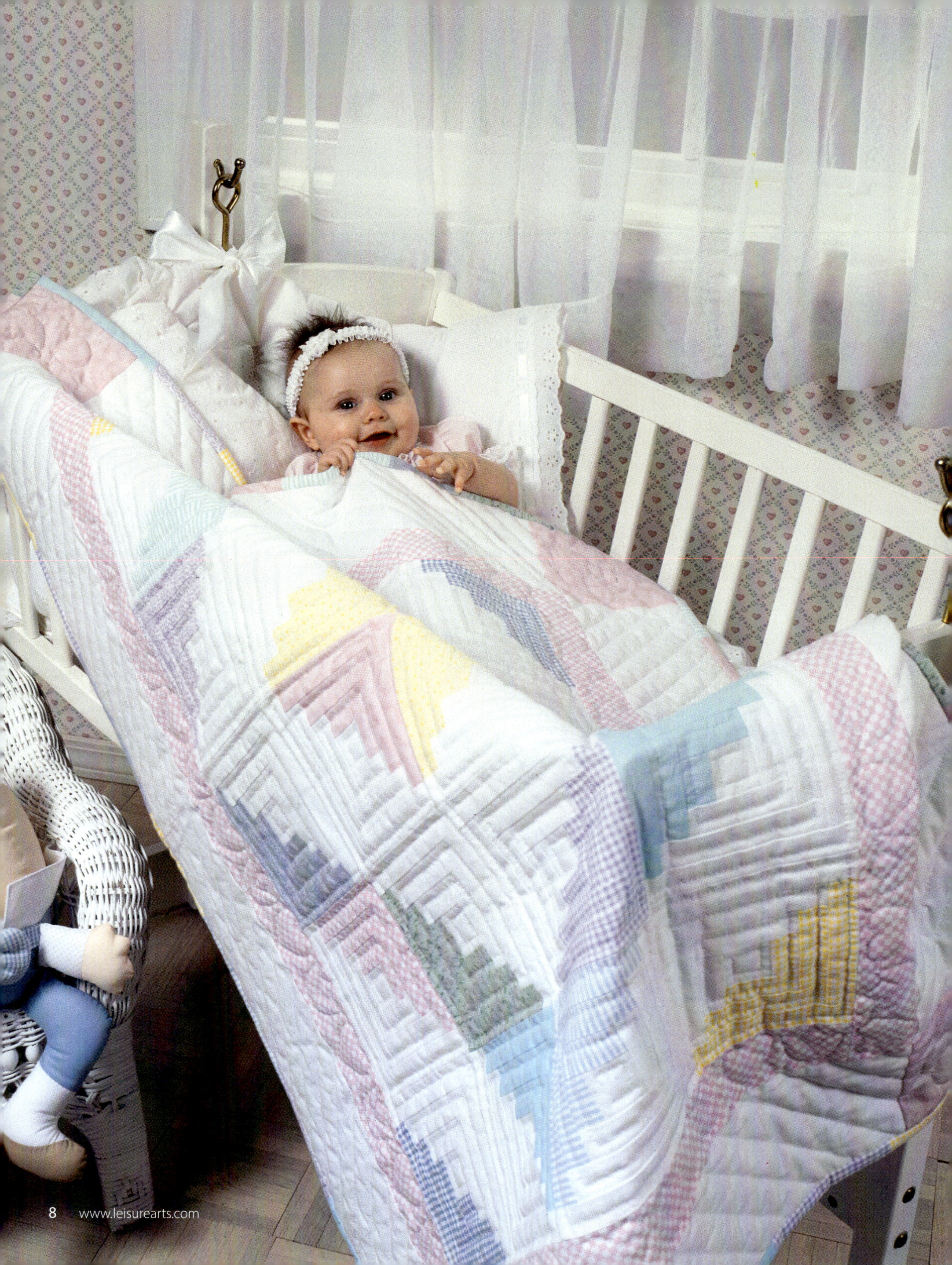

Log Cabin Lullaby

These pretty pastels keep Baby cozy! The Log Cabin block is an all-time favorite with quilters, and the trim-as-you-go method reduces the worry of working with small fabric pieces. A quilting motif of hearts and flowers adds an extra touch of sweetness to the border.

YARDAGE REQUIREMENTS

Yardage is based on 43"/44" (109 cm/112 cm) wide fabric.

$1^1/_2$ yds (1.4 m) of white solid fabric

$^1/_2$ yd (46 cm) of pink check fabric

$^1/_4$ yd (23 cm) of pink print fabric

$^1/_4$ yd (23 cm) each of yellow print, yellow check, blue print, blue stripe, blue check, purple print, purple check, green print, green stripe, and aqua print

$3^1/_4$ yds (3 m) of fabric for backing

You will also need:
46" x $57^1/_2$ " (117 cm x 146 cm) piece of batting

FINISHED BLOCK SIZE:
$5^3/_4$" x $5^3/_4$" (15 cm x 15 cm)

FINISHED QUILT SIZE:
38" x $49^1/_2$" (97 cm x 126 cm)

CUTTING THE PIECES

Follow Rotary Cutting, page 56, to cut fabric. Cut all strips across the selvage-to-selvage width of the fabric.

All measurements include $^1/_4$" seam allowances.

From white solid fabric:
- Cut 2 strips $1^3/_4$"w. From these strips, cut 24 squares $1^3/_4$" x $1^3/_4$".
- Cut 18 strips $1^1/_4$"w.
- Cut 2 side outer borders $5^1/_2$" x 39".
- Cut 2 top/bottom outer borders $5^1/_2$" x $27^1/_2$".

From pink check fabric:
- Cut 2 side inner borders $2^1/_2$" x 39".
- Cut 2 top/bottom inner borders $2^1/_2$" x $23^1/_2$".
- Cut 2 strips $1^1/_4$"w.

From pink print fabric:
- Cut 1 strip $5^1/_2$"w. From this strip, cut 4 corner squares $5^1/_2$" x $5^1/_2$".
- Cut 2 strips $1^1/_4$"w.

From yellow print, yellow check, blue print, blue stripe, blue check, purple print, purple check, green print, green stripe, and aqua print:
- Cut 2 strips $1^1/_4$"w from each fabric.

ASSEMBLING THE QUILT TOP

Follow Machine Piecing, page 57, and Pressing, page 57. Use a $^1/_4$" seam allowance.

1. Place 1 pink check strip on 1 square with right sides together and raw edges matching. Stitch as shown in Fig. 1. Trim strip even with square (Fig. 2); press open (Fig. 3).

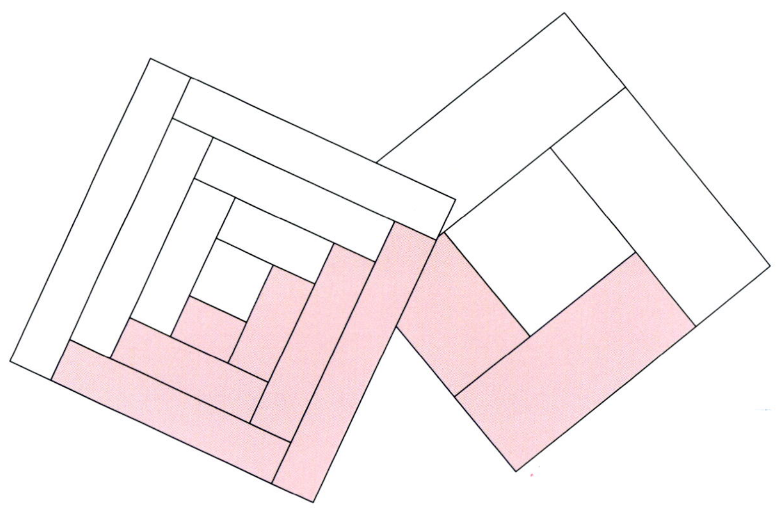

Fig. 1

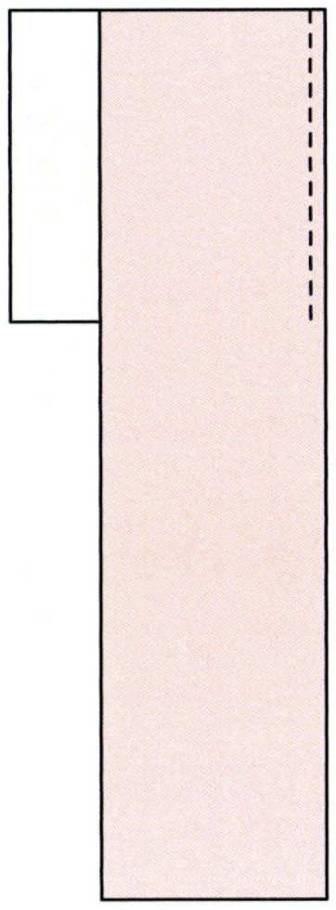

Fig. 2

Fig. 3

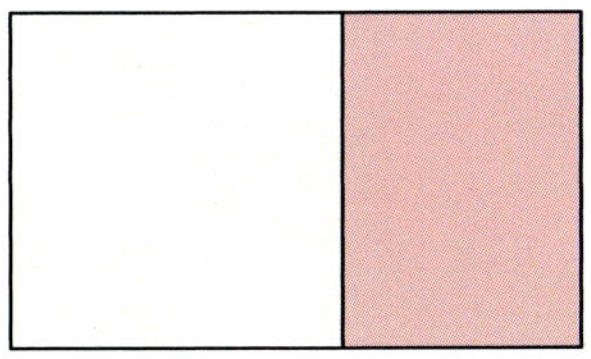

2. Turn square 1/4 turn to the left and repeat Step 1 to add the next "log" as shown in Figs. 4–6.

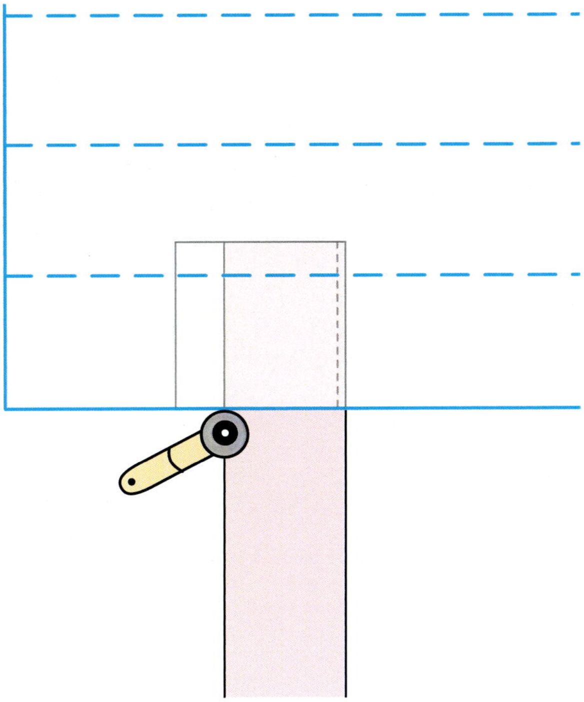

Fig. 4

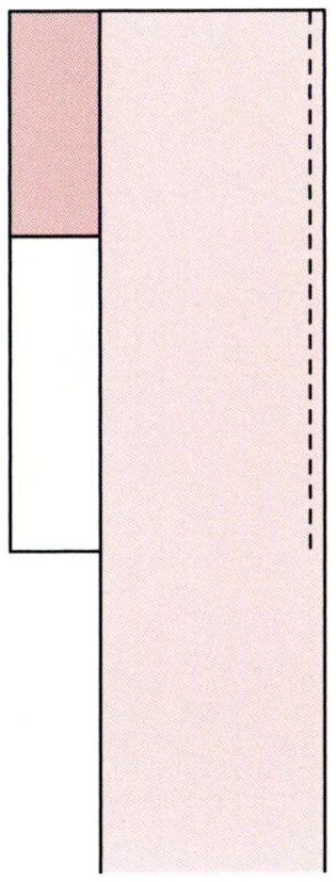

Fig. 5

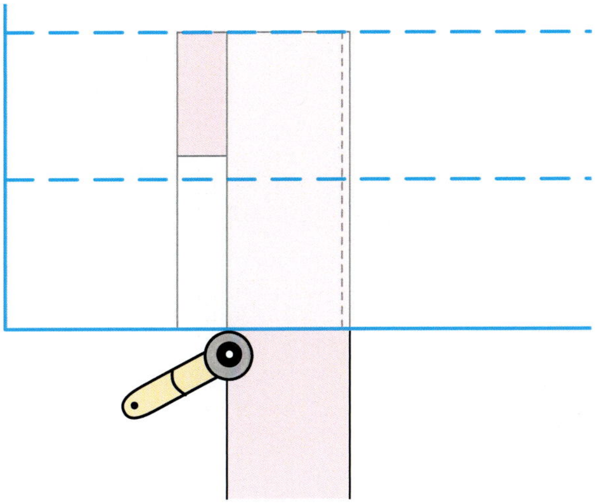

Fig. 6

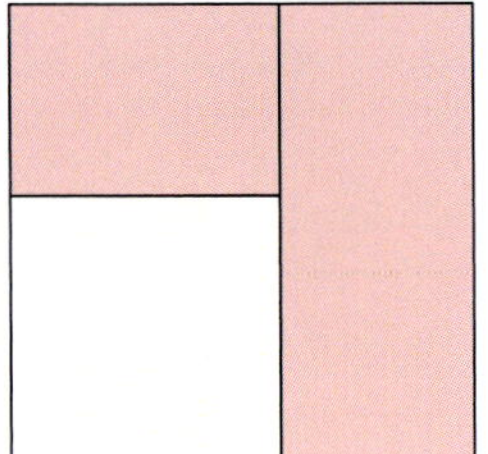

3. Repeat Step 2 to add white strips to remaining 2 sides of square (Fig. 7).

Fig. 7

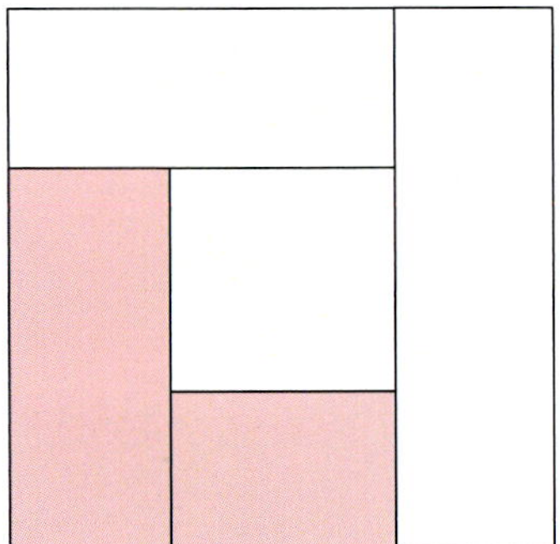

4. Continue adding strips, alternating 2 pink check strips and 2 white strips until there are 3 strips on each side of square to make Block. Make 2 Blocks using pink check and white strips.

Block

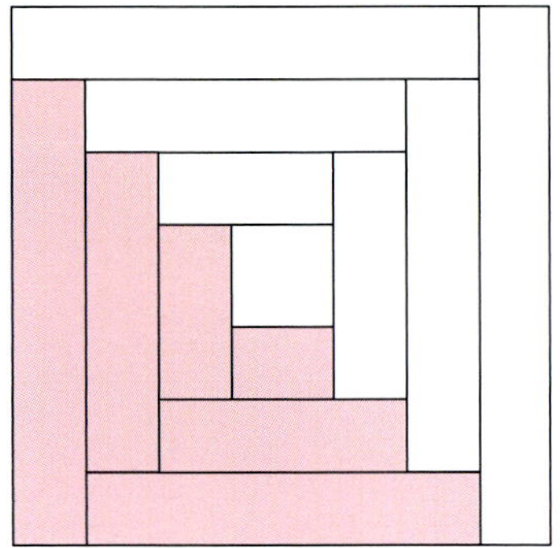

5. Using remaining strips, repeat Steps 1–4 to make a total of 24 Blocks (2 Blocks using each color print, check, or stripe).
6. Referring to Quilt Top Diagram, for color placement, sew Blocks together into rows. Sew rows together to make center section of quilt top.
7. Sew top, bottom, then side inner borders to center section.
8. Sew 1 corner square to each end of each side outer border. Sew top, bottom, then side outer borders to center section to complete Quilt Top.

COMPLETING THE QUILT

1. Follow Quilting, page 60, to mark, layer, and quilt, using Quilting Diagram as a suggestion. Our quilt is hand quilted.
2. Follow Making A Hanging Sleeve, page 64, if a sleeve is desired.
3. To make pieced binding, cut remaining scraps of print, check, and stripe fabrics into pieces $2^1/_2$"w and varying in length from $3^1/_2$" to $6^1/_2$". Sew pieces together along $2^1/_2$"w edges to make 2 top/bottom binding pieces 40"l and 2 side binding pieces 52"l. Follow Attaching Binding with Overlapped Corners, page 68, to bind quilt.

Quilting Diagram

Quilt Top Diagram

Bella Baby

This quilt is a cozy companion for your little one. Featuring a charming mix of floral and striped fabrics, it showcases playful four-patch blocks framed with soft sashings. Adorable corner appliqués add charm, making it perfect for cuddles and tummy time. Wrap your baby in the warmth and love of Bella Baby, where every stitch promises comfort and joy.

Design by Amy Hamberlin

YARDAGE REQUIREMENTS

Yardage is based on 43"/44" (109 cm/112 cm) wide fabric.

40 squares 5" x 5" (13 cm x 13 cm) OR 1 Charm Pack with at least 40 squares

5/8 yd (57 cm) of white print fabric for sashing and inner borders

3/4 yd (69 cm) of pink stripe fabric for outer borders

Scraps of fabrics for appliqués

2 7/8 yds (2.6 m) of fabric for backing

3/4 yd (69 cm) of fabric for binding

You will also need:

50" x 50" (127 cm x 127 cm) piece of batting

3 1/2 yds (3.2 m) of super jumbo rickrack

1/2 yd (46 cm) of paper-backed fusible web

FINISHED BLOCK SIZE:
4" x 4"
(10 cm x 25 cm)

FINISHED QUILT SIZE:
42" x 42"
(107 cm x 107cm)

CUTTING THE PIECES

Follow Rotary Cutting, page 56, to cut fabric. Cut borders across the selvage-to-selvage width of the fabric. Borders are cut longer than necessary and will be trimmed to fit quilt top center.

All measurements include 1/4" seam allowances.

From 40 squares 5" x 5" OR Charm Pack:

- Choose 36 squares and cut each in half to make 72 rectangles 2 1/2" x 5". Reserve the remaining squares for large and small center appliqués.

From white print fabric:

- Cut 2 top/bottom inner borders 35 1/2" x 1 1/2" .
- Cut 2 side inner borders 33 1/2" x 1 1/2".
- Cut 5 long sashings 29 1/2" x 1 1/2".
- Cut 4 strips 1 1/2" w. From these strips, cut 30 short sashings 1 1/2" x 4 1/2".

From pink stripe fabric:

- Cut 2 top/bottom outer borders 5 1/2" x width of fabric.
- Cut 2 side outer borders 35 1/2" x 5 1/2".

CUTTING THE APPLIQUES

Follow Preparing Fusible Appliqués, page 58, to use patterns on page 19.

Note: Appliqué patterns are printed in reverse.

From squares and scraps for appliqués:

- Cut 2 left swirls.
- Cut 2 right swirls.
- Cut 4 petals.
- Cut 2 large centers.
- Cut 2 small centers.

ASSEMBLING THE QUILT TOP CENTER

Follow Machine Piecing, page 57, and Pressing, page 57. Match right sides and use a $^{1}/_{4}$" seam allowance. Set seams and press seam allowances to darker fabric throughout construction.

1. Sew 2 rectangles together to make Unit 1. Make 36 Unit 1's.
2. Cutting perpendicular to the seam, cut each Unit 1 in half to make 72 Unit 2's.
3. Sew 2 assorted Unit 2's together to make a Four-Patch Block. Make 36 Four-Patch Blocks.

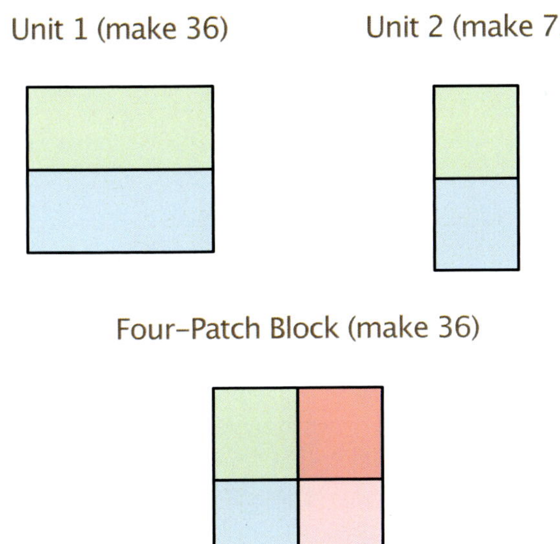

4. Sew 6 Four-Patch Blocks and 5 short sashings together to make a Row. Make 6 Rows.
5. Sew 6 Rows and 5 long sashings together to make Quilt Top Center.
6. Cut four 31" lengths of rickrack. Sewing through middle of rickrack, sew rickrack $^{1}/_{4}$" from top and bottom edge of Quilt Top Center. Repeat to sew rickrack to each side of Quilt Top Center. Trim any rickrack hanging off the edges of the Quilt Top Center.

ADDING THE BORDERS

1. Measure through the Quilt Top Center from top to bottom. Trim 2 side inner borders to the determined measurement. Sew side inner borders to Quilt Top Center.
2. Measure through the center of the quilt from side to side (including borders). Trim 2 top/bottom inner borders to the determined measurement. Sew top/bottom inner borders to Quilt Top.
3. Repeat Steps 1–2 to add outer borders to Quilt Top.

APPLIQUEING THE QUILT TOP

1. Fuse appliqués to 2 opposite corners of quilt top.
2. Follow Machine Blanket Stitch Appliqué, page 58, to stitch appliqués in place. If you don't have a blanket stitch on your machine, use a comparable stitch or a zigzag stitch.

COMPLETING THE QUILT

1. Follow Quilting, page 60, to mark, layer, and quilt as desired. Our quilt is machine quilted with meandering swirls. We also quilted the wavy edge of the rickrack in place.
2. If desired, follow Making A Hanging Sleeve, page 64, to add hanging sleeve.
3. Cut a 24" square of binding fabric. Follow Binding, page 65, to bind quilt using $2^{1}/_{2}$"w continuous bias binding with mitered corners.

SETTING SEAMS

Before pressing seam allowances to one side, set your seams by gently pressing the length of the seam. After setting your seam, press the seam allowances toward the darkest fabric.

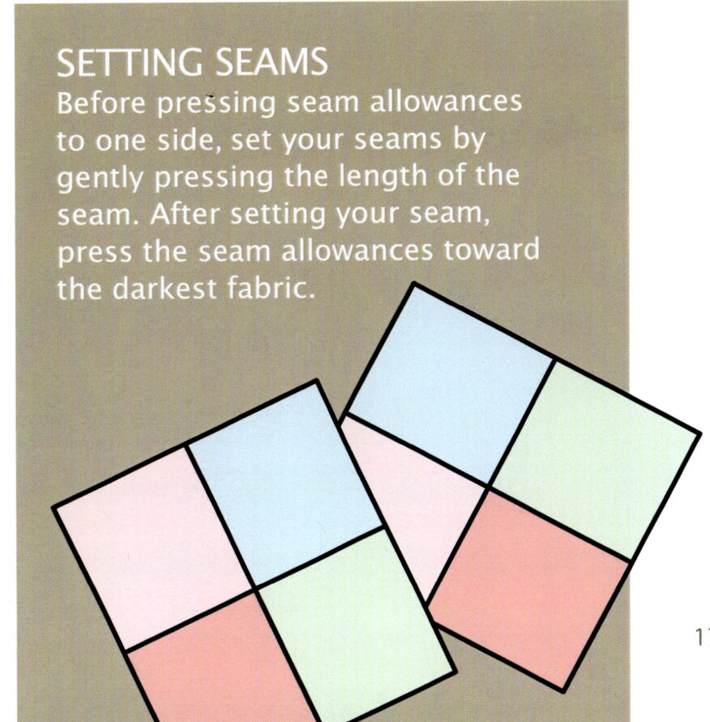

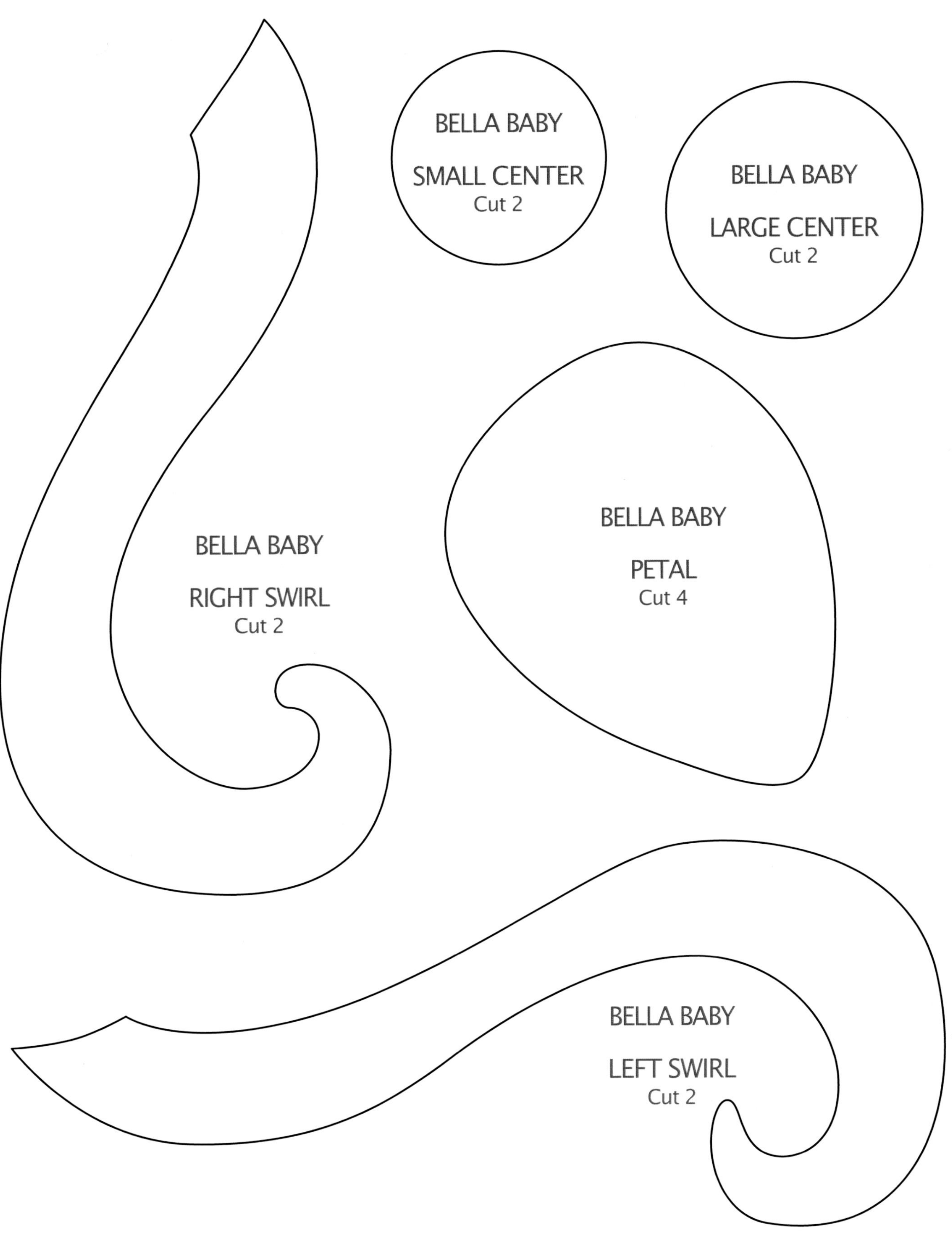
BELLA BABY
SMALL CENTER
Cut 2
BELLA BABY
LARGE CENTER
Cut 2
BELLA BABY
RIGHT SWIRL
Cut 2
BELLA BABY
PETAL
Cut 4
BELLA BABY
LEFT SWIRL
Cut 2

Islandar IV

Sailboat

Quilted "waves" keep a flotilla of sailboats afloat on this sweet little blanket. The boats are composed of triangle-squares and rectangles for quick piecing. To ensure that your handiwork is long-wearing and destined to become an heirloom, the double-fold binding provides an extra layer of fabric along the edges of the quilt.

YARDAGE REQUIREMENTS

Yardage is based on 43"/44" (109 cm/112 cm) wide fabric with a usable width of 40" (102 cm).

$2^5/_8$ yds (2.4 m) of blue solid fabric

$1^1/_2$ yds (1.4 m) of white solid fabric

$4^1/_2$ yds (4.1 m) of fabric for backing

$^7/_8$ yd (80 cm) of fabric for binding

55" x 80" (140 cm x 203 cm) piece of batting

FINISHED BLOCK SIZE:
10" x 10" (25 cm x 25 cm)

FINISHED QUILT SIZE:
47" x 72" (119 cm x 183 cm)

To bring our vintage 1960's Sailboat quilt more in line with today's quick methods and standards, our instructions include simplified piecing and more durable double-fold binding.

CUTTING THE PIECES

Follow Rotary Cutting, page 56, to cut fabric. Cut all strips across the selvage-to-selvage width of the fabric unless otherwise indicated.

All measurements include $^1/_4$" seam allowances.

From blue solid fabric:

- Cut 5 strips $3^1/_2$"w. From these strips, cut 45 squares $3^1/_2$ x $3^1/_2$".
- Cut 2 lengthwise side borders 5" x $71^1/_2$".
- Cut 2 lengthwise sashing strips 4" x $71^1/_2$".
- From remaining fabric width, cut 4 strips 3"w. From these strips, cut 15 rectangles 3" x $5^1/_2$".
- From remaining fabric width, cut 9 strips 4" wide. From these strips, cut 18 sashing rectangles 4" x $10^1/_2$".

From white solid fabric:

- Cut 5 strips $3^1/_2$"w. From these strips, cut 45 squares $3^1/_2$" x $3^1/_2$".
- Cut 5 strips 3"w. From these strips, cut 30 rectangles 3" x $5^1/_2$".
- Cut 5 strips 3" wide. From these strips, cut 15 large rectangles 3" x $10^1/_2$".

Quilt Top Diagram

ASSEMBLING THE QUILT TOP

Follow Machine Piecing, page 57, and Pressing, page 57. Use a $^1/_4$" seam allowance.

1. Draw a diagonal line on wrong side of each white solid square. With right sides together place 1 white solid square on top of 1 blue solid square. Stitch seam $^1/_4$" from each side of drawn line (Fig. 1).

Fig. 1

2. Cut along drawn line and press seam allowances to darker fabric to make 2 Triangle-Squares. Make 90 Triangle-Squares. Trim each Triangle-Square to 3" x 3".

Triangle-Squares (make 90)

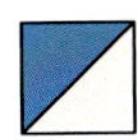

3. Sew 4 triangle-squares together to make Unit 1. Make 15 Unit 1's.

Unit 1 (make 15)

4. Sew 1 Unit 1 and 2 white solid rectangles together to make Unit 2. Make 15 Unit 2's.

Unit 2 (make 15)

5. Sew 2 triangle-squares and 1 blue solid rectangle together to make Unit 3. Make 15 Unit 3's.

Unit 3 (make 15)

6. Sew 1 Unit 2, 1 Unit 3, and 1 large rectangle together to make Block. Make 15 Blocks.

Block (make 15)

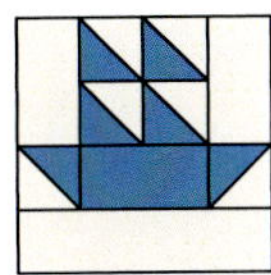

7. Sew 6 sashing rectangles and 5 Blocks together to make 1 vertical Row. Make 3 Rows.

Row (make 3)

8. Referring to Quilt Top Diagram, sew 3 Rows and 2 sashing strips together to make center section of quilt top.

9. Sew side borders to center section to complete Quilt Top.

COMPLETING THE QUILT

1. Follow Quilting, page 60, to mark, layer, and quilt, using Quilting Diagram as a suggestion. Our quilt is hand quilted.
2. Follow Making A Hanging Sleeve, page 64, if hanging sleeve is desired.
3. Cut a 27" square of binding fabric. Follow Making Continuous Bias Strip Binding, page 65, to make $2^1/_2$"w bias binding.
4. Follow Attaching Binding With Mitered Corners, page 66, to attach binding to quilt.

Quilting Diagram

Giggles

Every baby has his own unique way of laughing, whether it's a coo, a gurgle, or a chortle. However he expresses it, the sweetest part of any baby's laugh is the irrepressible glee that inspired it. This little quilt captures that joy in its easy strips and prairie points. This giggle-getter is also stunning in pink.

Design by Me & My Sister Designs • Barbara Groves & Mary Jacobson

YARDAGE REQUIREMENTS

Yardage is based on 43"/44" (109 cm/112 cm) wide fabric.

- $^3/_4$ yd (69 cm) of red print fabric
- $^3/_8$ yd (34 cm) of multi-color print fabric
- $^1/_4$ yd (23 cm) of blue print fabric
- $^5/_8$ yd (57 cm) of multi-color stripe fabric
- $^7/_8$ yd (80 cm) of multi-color novelty print fabric
- $^3/_8$ yd (34 cm) of fabric for binding
- $3^1/_4$ yds (3 m) of fabric for backing

You will also need:

- 46" x 57" (117 cm x 145 cm) rectangle of batting
- Four 1" (25 mm) buttons*
- White embroidery floss or 1 yd (91 cm) of $^1/_8$" (3 mm) wide satin ribbon

*Buttons can be a choking hazard for babies or small children. Make sure they are securely attached.

FINISHED QUILT SIZE:
$37^3/_4$" x $48^3/_4$" (96 cm x 124 cm)

CUTTING OUT THE PIECES

Follow Rotary Cutting, page 56, to cut fabric. Cut all strips from the selvage-to-selvage width of the fabric. Borders lengths are exact.

All measurements include $^1/_4$" seam allowances.

From red print fabric:

- Cut 4 strips 4"w. From these strips, cut 40 squares 4" x 4".
- Cut 1 center rectangle $5^1/_2$" x $16^1/_2$".

From multi-color print fabric:

- Cut 2 strips $4^1/_2$"w. From these strips, cut 2 first round sides $4^1/_2$" x $16^1/_2$" and 2 first round top/bottoms $4^1/_2$" x $13^1/_2$".

From blue print fabric:

- Cut 3 strips $2^1/_2$"w. From these strips, cut 2 second round sides $2^1/_2$" x $24^1/_2$" and 2 second round top/bottoms $2^1/_2$" x $17^1/_2$".

From multi-color stripe fabric:

- Cut 2 third round sides $4^1/_2$" x $28^1/_2$".
- Cut 2 third round top/bottoms $4^1/_2$" x $25^1/_2$".

From multi-color novelty print fabric:

- Cut 2 side borders $6^1/_2$" x $36^1/_2$".
- Cut 2 top/bottom borders $6^1/_2$" x $37^1/_2$".

From fabric for binding:

- Cut 5 binding strips $2^1/_4$"w.

MAKING THE QUILT TOP CENTER

Refer to photo and follow Piecing, page 57, and Pressing, page 57, to make quilt top center. Use 1/4" seam allowances throughout.

1. Sew first round sides to center rectangle, and then add first round top/bottoms to complete first round.
2. Sew second round sides to first round, and then add second round top/bottoms to complete second round.
3. Sew third round sides to second round, and then add third round top/bottoms to complete quilt top center.

ADDING THE PRAIRIE POINTS

1. For each Prairie Point, fold 1 square in half diagonally with wrong sides together and then fold in half again; press. Make 40 Prairie Points.
   Tip: Spraying the squares with temporary fabric adhesive before folding will help prevent slipping.
2. Matching right sides and raw edges, evenly space and overlap 12 Prairie Points on each side of quilt top center and 8 Prairie Points on top and bottom of quilt top center. Points should be facing toward the center of the quilt and should meet in the corners without overlap (Fig. 1). Pin and then baste Prairie Points in place

Fig. 1

ADDING THE BORDERS

1. Matching centers and corners, sew side borders to quilt top center.
2. Matching centers and corners, sew top/bottom borders to quilt top center.

COMPLETING THE QUILT

1. Follow Quilting, page 60, to mark, layer, and quilt as desired. Quilt shown is machine quilted. A star with swirling trails is quilted in the center rectangle, straight lines radiating from the center rectangle are quilted in the first round, and swirls are quilted in the second round. Overlapping scallops are quilted from the third round/border seams into the third round. The borders have straight and curved lines quilted around the Prairie Points and in the corners.
2. Follow Making a Hanging Sleeve, page 64, if a hanging sleeve is desired.
3. Follow Binding, page 65, to make and then attach straight-grain binding with mitered corners.
4. Use 12 strands of embroidery floss or satin ribbon to tie buttons to quilt. Trim ends as desired.

I Love You This Much

The title "I Love You This Much" truly embodies the warmth and affection that a baby quilt represents. It's a heartfelt expression that makes the quilt not just a functional item but also a cherished keepsake. The combination of pinks, blues, purples, yellows, and greens, will add a lovely mix of texture and color. Adding some playful quilting patterns, like butterflies inside the hearts, will also complement the overall design beautifully.

Design by Sue Marsh for Whistlepig Creek Productions

YARDAGE REQUIREMENTS

Yardage is based on 43"/44" (109 cm/112 cm) wide fabric with a usable width of 40" (102 cm).

A Layer Cake includes a variety of 10" x 10" (25 cm x 25 cm) squares.

A Twice the Charm Roll includes a variety of $5\frac{1}{2}$" x 22" (14 cm x 56 cm) rectangles.

1 Layer Cake or 13 [25, 32] squares 10" x 10" (25 cm x 25 cm) or 1 Twice the Charm Roll or 13 [25, 32] strips $5\frac{1}{2}$" x 22" (14 cm x 56 cm)

$\frac{1}{2}$ yd (46 cm) [1 yd (91 cm), $1\frac{1}{8}$ yds (1 m)] of white polka dot fabric for blocks

$\frac{3}{4}$ yd (69 cm) [$1\frac{1}{4}$ yds (1.1 m), $1\frac{1}{4}$ yds (1.1 m)] of white print fabric for setting triangles

$\frac{3}{4}$ yd (69 cm) [$1\frac{1}{4}$ yds (1.1 m), $1\frac{3}{8}$ yds (1.3 m)] of dark purple print fabric for sashings and inner border

$1\frac{1}{8}$ yds (1 m) [$1\frac{1}{4}$ yds (1.1 m), $1\frac{3}{8}$ yds (1.3 m)] of pink print fabric for outer border

$3\frac{5}{8}$ yds (3.3 m) [$4\frac{1}{2}$ yds (4.1 m), $5\frac{1}{4}$ yds (4.8 m)] of fabric for backing

$\frac{5}{8}$ yd (57 cm) [$\frac{5}{8}$ yd (57 cm), $\frac{3}{4}$ yd (69 cm)] of fabric for binding

You will also need:

65" x 65" (165 cm x 165 cm) [79" x 79" (201 cm x 201 cm), 79" x 93" (201 cm x 236 cm)] piece of batting

FINISHED CRIB QUILT SIZE: $56\frac{7}{8}$" x $56\frac{7}{8}$" (144 cm x 144 cm)
FINISHED ALTERNATE LAP QUILT SIZE: 71" x 71" (180 cm x 180 cm)
FINISHED ALTERNATE TWIN QUILT SIZE: 71" x $85\frac{1}{8}$" (180 cm x 216 cm)
FINISHED BLOCK SIZE: 9" x 9" (23 cm x 23 cm)

Note: Instructions are written for the crib size quilt shown in the photo, page 32, with alternative lap and twin sizes in [ ]. Instructions will be easier to follow if you circle all the numbers pertaining to your desired size quilt. If only one number is given, it applies to all sizes.

CUTTING THE PIECES

Follow Rotary Cutting, page 56, to cut fabric. Cut all strips from the selvage-to-selvage width of the fabric.

All measurements include $\frac{1}{4}$" seam allowances.

From each of 13 [25, 32] squares or strips:

- Cut 1 rectangle 5" x $9\frac{1}{2}$".
- Cut 1 large square 5" x 5".

From white polka dot fabric:

- Cut 2 [4, 4] strips 5" wide. From these strips, cut 13 [25, 32] large background squares 5" x 5".
- Cut 3 [5, 7] strips 2" wide. From these strips, cut 52 [100, 128] small background squares 2" x 2".

From white print fabric:

- Cut 1 [2, 2] strip(s) $15\frac{1}{2}$ wide. From this (these) strip(s), cut 2 [3, 4] squares $15\frac{1}{2}$" x $15\frac{1}{2}$". Cut squares twice diagonally to make 8 [12, 16 (you will use 14)] side setting triangles.
- Cut 1 strip $8\frac{3}{4}$" wide. From this strip, cut 2 squares $8\frac{3}{4}$" x $8\frac{3}{4}$". Cut squares once diagonally to make 4 corner setting triangles.

From dark purple print fabric:

- Cut 16 [25, 30] sashing and inner border strips $1\frac{1}{2}$" wide.

From pink print fabric:

- Cut 6 [7, 8] outer border strips $5\frac{1}{2}$" wide.

From fabric for binding:

- Cut 7 [8, 9] binding strips $2\frac{1}{2}$" wide.

MAKING THE BLOCKS

Follow Piecing, page 57, and Pressing, page 57, to make quilt top. Use $^1/_4$" seam allowances throughout.

1. Draw a diagonal line on wrong side of each small background square.
2. Matching right sides, place 1 small background square on 2 adjacent corners of 1 rectangle and stitch along drawn line; trim $^1/_4$" from stitching line (Fig. 1); press open to make Unit 1. Make 13 [25, 32] Unit 1's.

Fig. 1

Unit 1 (make 13 [25, 32])

3. In the same manner, sew 2 small background squares to adjacent corners of 1 large square to make Unit 2. Make 13 [25, 32] Unit 2's.

Unit 2 (make 13 [25, 32])

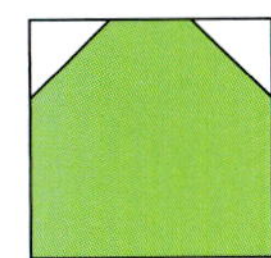

4. Sew 1 Unit 2 and 1 large background square together to make Unit 3. Make 13 [25, 32] Unit 3's.

Unit 3 (make 13 [25, 32])

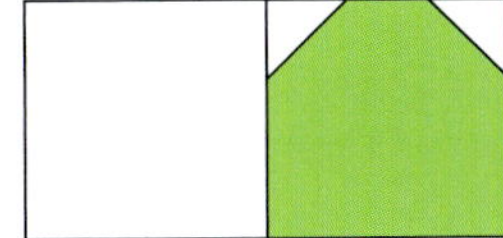

5. Sew 1 Unit 1 and 1 Unit 3 with matching fabrics together to make Block. Block should measure $9^1/_2$" x $9^1/_2$" including seam allowances. Make 13 [25, 32] Blocks.

Block (make 13 [25, 32])

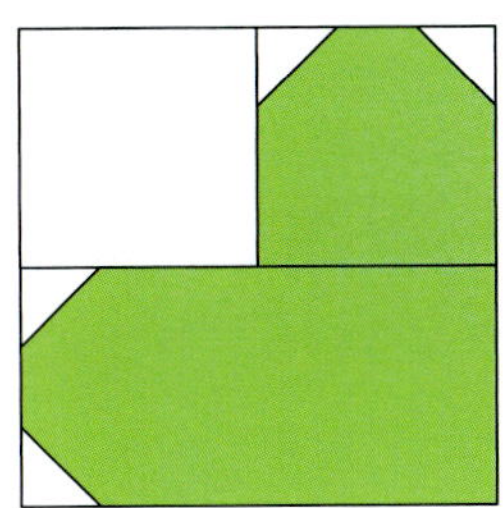

CUTTING THE SASHINGS

1. Using sashings and inner border strips and piecing as needed, follow table to cut sashings. Set remainder of strips aside for inner borders.

Cut Length	Number of Sashings		
	Crib	Lap	Twin
$81^1/_2$"	-	-	1
$71^1/_2$"	-	2	2
$51^1/_2$"	2	2	2
$31^1/_2$"	2	2	2
$11^1/_2$"	2	2	2
$9^1/_2$"	18	32	40

ASSEMBLING THE QUILT TOP CENTER

Refer to Assembly Diagram, page 33 [34, 35], to assemble quilt top. Measurements on diagram indicate cut sizes which include seam allowances.

1. Sew Blocks, sashings, and side setting triangles together to make diagonal Rows.
2. Sew Rows together and then add corner setting triangles to make Quilt Top Center. Leaving $^1/_4$" seam allowances beyond corner points of sashings, trim outer edges as needed. Quilt Top Center should measure approximately $44^3/_8$" x $44^3/_8$ [$58^1/_2$" x $58^1/_2$", $58^1/_2$" x $72^5/_8$"] including seam allowances.

ADDING THE BORDERS

1. Sew strips for inner borders (set aside earlier) together end to end. Follow Adding Squared Borders, page 59, to sew side and then top/bottom inner borders to Quilt Top Center.
2. In the same manner, use outer border strips to sew outer borders to Quilt Top.

COMPLETING THE QUILT

1. Follow Quilting, page 60, to mark, layer, and quilt as desired. Quilt shown is machine quilted. A butterfly motif is quilted in each block and a flower motif is quilted in each setting triangle. A continuous loop pattern is quilted in the sashings and inner border and a continuous flower pattern is quilted in the outer border.
2. Follow Making a Hanging Sleeve, page 64, if a hanging sleeve is desired.
3. Use binding strips and follow Binding, page 65, to make and attach straight-grain binding with mitered corners.

CRIB QUILT TOP DIAGRAM

CRIB QUILT ASSEMBLY DIAGRAM

LAP QUILT ASSEMBLY DIAGRAM

TWIN QUILT ASSEMBLY DIAGRAM

Dr. Seuss's ABC
Ten Apples Up On Top!

All Aboard

QUILT TOP CENTER

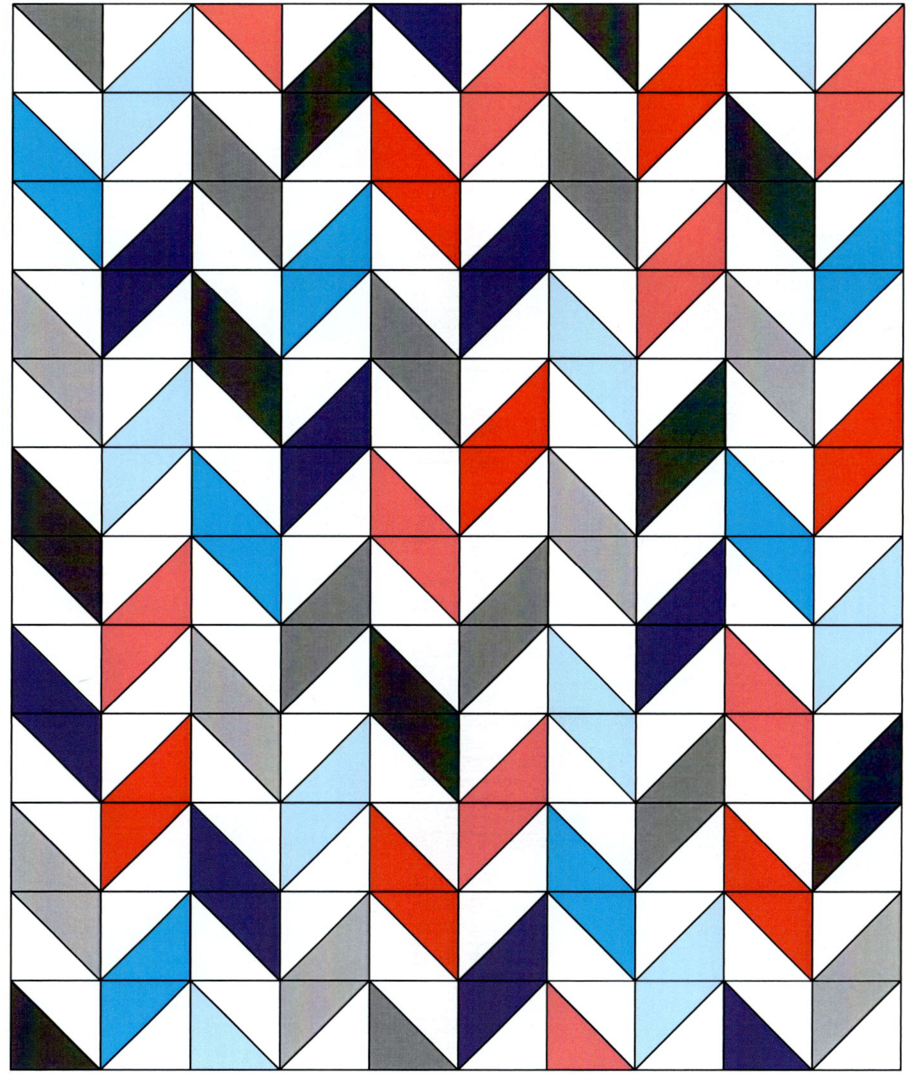

This quilt is a charming addition to your child's nursery. With a delightful red, white, and blue palette, it features half-square triangles and bold patterns. More than just functional, the "All Aboard" quilt is a treasured keepsake for countless adventures. Wrap your little one in warmth and love, perfect for snuggles and nap times.

Design by Susan Emory

YARDAGE REQUIREMENTS

Yardage is based on 43"/44" wide fabric with a usable width of 40".

Fat quarters are approximately 22" x 18".

Fat quarter each of 8 assorted prints and solids

1/4 yds (1.1m) of white fabric for background

3/4 yd (69cm) of fabric for border

3 5/8 yds (3.3m) of fabric for backing

3/4 yd (69cm) of fabric for binding

You will also need:
56" x 64" (142 cm x 163cm) piece of batting

FINISHED QUILT SIZE:
48" x 56"
(122 cm x 142 cm)

CUTTING THE PIECES

Follow Rotary Cutting, page 56, to cut fabric. WOF = width of fabric from selvage to selvage. For fat quarters, cut strips parallel to the long edge. Border is cut exact length.

All measurements include 1/4" seam allowances.

From each of 8 fat quarters:

- Cut [8] 5" squares.

From background fabric:

- Cut [8] 5" x WOF strip; from these strips, cut [60] 5" squares.

From fabric for border:

- Cut [5] 4 1/2" x WOF strips.

From fabric for binding:

- Cut [1] 25" square.

QUILT TOP

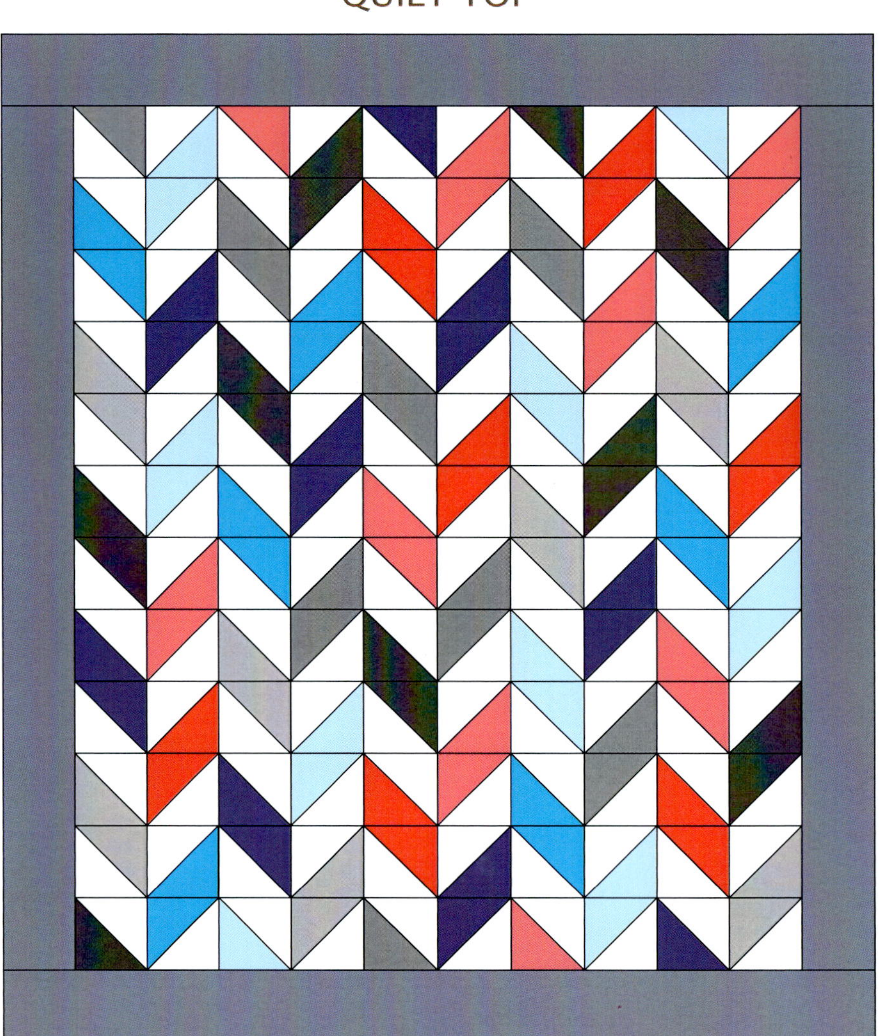

ASSEMBLING THE QUILT TOP

Follow Machine Piecing and Pressing, page 57, to make quilt top. Refer to Quilt Top for assembly. Use $^{1}/_{4}$" seam allowances throughout.

1. Draw a diagonal line on the wrong side of [60] 5" background squares. With right sides together, place a 5" background square on top of a 5" print square. Stitch $^{1}/_{4}$" on each side of drawn line (Fig. 1). Cut along drawn line (Fig. 2) and press toward darker fabric to make a Half-Square Triangle. Trim half-square triangle to $4^{1}/_{2}$" square. Repeat with remaining 5" squares to yield a total of [120] half-square triangles.
   Note: You will have [4] extra 5" print squares.

2. Arrange all half-square triangles as shown in Fig. 3; rearrange as desired to balance colors. Sew together in horizontal rows. Press each row of blocks in the opposite direction from the row before. Sew rows together and press to complete Quilt Top Center.

3. Trim selvages from [5] $4^{1}/_{2}$" x WOF border strips and sew together end to end.

4. Cut [4] strips $48^{1}/_{2}$" long. Sew a border to each side of quilt. Press toward border strips.

5. Sew a border to top and bottom of quilt. Press toward border strips to complete Quilt Top.

Fig. 1

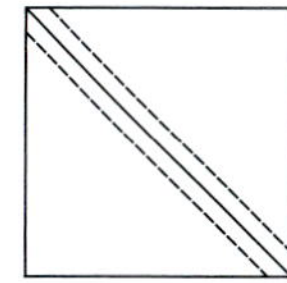

Fig. 2

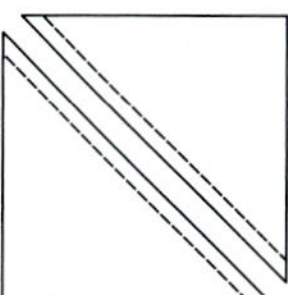

Half-Square Triangle (make 120)

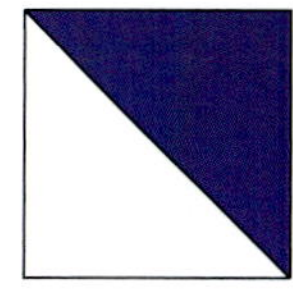

Fig. 3

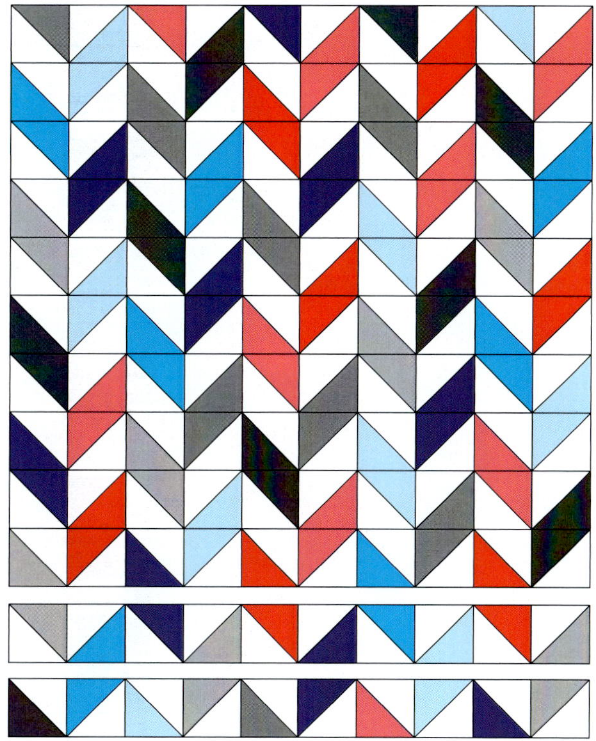

COMPLETING THE QUILT

1. Follow Quilting, page 60, to mark, layer, and quilt as desired. Quilt shown is quilted with an allover wave pattern with randomly spaced anchors.

2. Follow Making a Hanging Sleeve, page 64, if a hanging sleeve is desired.

3. Use square and follow Making Continuous Bias Strip Binding, page 65, to make binding. Follow Attaching Binding with Mitered Corners, page 66, to bind quilt.

Playdate

Oh, how much that wee one loves to play! And what play date wouldn't be more fun on a quilt featuring a bold butterfly print? Use a big square of any happy fabric for the center of your quilt, and the rest of the piecing will go quickly. This quilt is equally wonderful with a different fabric mix.

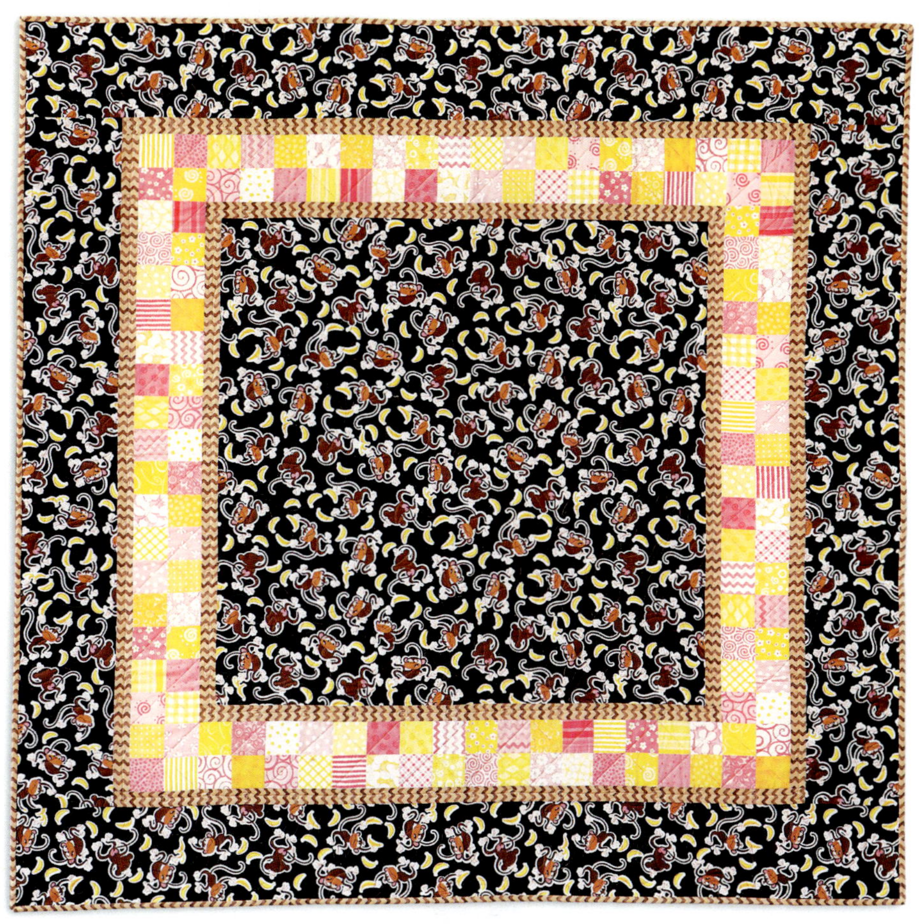

Design by Me & My Sister Designs • Barbara Groves & Mary Jacobson

YARDAGE REQUIREMENTS

Yardage is based on 43"/44" (109 cm/112 cm) wide fabric.

Charm Pack* with at least 36 squares

$2^{5}/_{8}$ yds (2.4 m) of blue novelty print fabric

$^{1}/_{2}$ yd (46 cm) of yellow print fabric

$^{1}/_{2}$ yd (46 cm) of fabric for binding

$3^{1}/_{2}$ yds (3.2 m) of fabric for backing

You will also need:

62" x 62" (157 cm x 157 cm) square of batting

*OR $^{7}/_{8}$ yds (80 cm) total of assorted print fabrics. Charm Packs (assortments of 5" x 5" squares) are available at most quilt stores.

FINISHED SIZE:

$54^{1}/_{4}$" x $54^{1}/_{4}$"
(138 cm x 138 cm)

CUTTING OUT THE PIECES

Follow Rotary Cutting, page 56, to cut fabric. Cut all strips from the selvage-to-selvage width of the fabric unless noted otherwise. Borders lengths are exact.

All measurements include $^{1}/_{4}$" seam allowances.

From assorted fabrics:

- Cut 36 squares 5" x 5" if not using Charm Pack.

From blue novelty print fabric:

- Cut 1 center square $30^{1}/_{2}$" x $30^{1}/_{2}$".
- Cut 2 lengthwise side fourth borders $6^{1}/_{4}$" x $42^{1}/_{2}$".
- Cut 2 lengthwise top/bottom fourth borders $6^{1}/_{4}$" x 54".

From yellow print fabric:

- Cut 2 side first borders $1^{1}/_{2}$" x $30^{1}/_{2}$".
- Cut 2 top/bottom first borders $1^{1}/_{2}$" x $32^{1}/_{2}$".
- Cut 2 side third borders $1^{1}/_{2}$" x $40^{1}/_{2}$", pieced as needed.
- Cut 2 top/bottom third borders $1^{1}/_{2}$" x $42^{1}/_{2}$", pieced as needed.

From fabric for binding:

- Cut 6 binding strips $2^{1}/_{2}$"w.

MAKING THE FOUR-PATCHES

Follow Piecing, page 57, and Pressing, page 57, to make Four-Patches. Use $^{1}/_{4}$" seam allowances throughout.

1. With right sides together, sew 2 squares together on opposite sides. Cut squares through center as shown in Fig. 1. Press open to make 2 Two-Patches. Make 36 Two-Patches.

Fig. 1

$2^{1}/_{2}$" $2^{1}/_{2}$"

Two-Patches
(make 36)

2. With right sides together and matching seams, layer 2 Two-Patches. Sew Two-Patches together on opposite sides perpendicular to seams previously made. Cut Two-Patches through center as shown in Fig. 2. Press open to make 2 Four Patches. Four-Patch should measure $4^1/_2$" x $4^1/_2$" including seam allowances. Make 36 Four-Patches.

Fig. 2

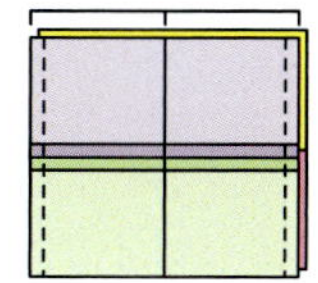

Four-Patches
(make 36)

MAKING THE SECOND BORDER

1. Sew 10 Four-Patches together to make top second border. Top second border should measure $4^1/_2$" x $40^1/_2$" including seam allowances. Repeat to make bottom second border.

Top/Bottom Second Border
(make 2)

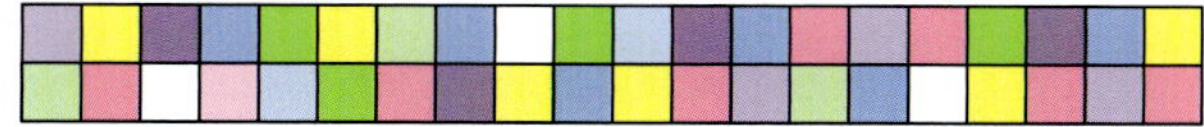

2. Sew 8 Four-Patches together to make side second border. Side second border should measure $4^1/_2$" x $32^1/_2$" including seam allowances. Make 2 side second borders.

Side Second Border
(make 2)

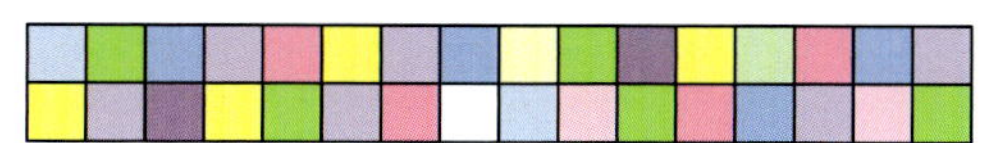

ASSEMBLING THE QUILT TOP

Refer to photo to assemble quilt top.

1. Matching centers and corners, sew side first borders to center square.
2. Matching centers and corners, sew top/bottom first borders to center square.
3. Repeat Steps 1 - 2 to add second, third, and fourth borders to quilt top.

COMPLETING THE QUILT

1. Follow Quilting, page 60, to mark, layer, and quilt as desired. Quilt shown is machine quilted with a free form pattern that resembles butterfly wings over the entire quilt.
2. Follow Making a Hanging Sleeve, page 64, if a hanging sleeve is desired.
3. Follow Binding, page 65, to make and then attach straight-grain binding with mitered corners.

Oh Baby

This delightful quilt showcases vibrant fish tails in pink, yellow, green, turquoise, blue, and purple against a crisp white background, creating a bright and cheerful place for your baby. Crafted from soft, cozy fabrics, the "Oh Baby" quilt is perfect for cuddles and playful moments.

Design by Susan Emory

YARDAGE REQUIREMENTS

Yardage is based on 43"/44" wide fabric with a usable width of 40".

$2^3/_4$ yds (2.5 m) of solid white fabric for background

$^1/_2$ yd (46 cm) each of 6 solid color fabrics

$3^3/_8$ yds (3.1 m) of fabric for backing

$^1/_2$ yd (46 cm) of fabric for binding

You will also need:

$6^1/_2$ yds (5.9 m) of 17" (43cm) wide paper-backed fusible web

56" x 60" (142 cm x 152 cm) piece of batting

Creative Grids™ Circle Savvy Ruler (optional)

template plastic and permanent marker (optional)

FINISHED QUILT SIZE: 48" x 52" (122 cm x 132 cm)

CUTTING THE PIECES

Follow Rotary Cutting, page 56, to cut fabric. WOF = cut strips across width of fabric from selvage to selvage.

All measurements include $^1/_4$" seam allowances.

From solid white fabric for background:

- Cut [20] $4^1/_2$" x WOF strips; from these strips, cut [156] $4^1/_2$" squares.

From each of 6 solid color fabrics:

- Cut [3] $4^1/_2$" x WOF strips; from these strips, cut [24] $4^1/_2$" squares.

From fabric for binding:

- Cut [6] $2^1/_2$" x WOF strips.

From paper-backed fusible web:

- Cut [144] $4^1/_2$" squares.

MAKING THE BLOCKS

Follow Machine Piecing and Pressing, page 57, to make quilt top. Use 1/4" seam allowances throughout. I recommend the Creative Grids™ Circle Savvy Ruler for cutting perfect circles but you may use the quarter-circle pattern, page 49, instead.

1. Set aside [12] 4 1/2" white background squares. These squares will not be fused or cut.
2. Following fusible web manufacturer's instructions, center and fuse [1] 4 1/2" square of fusible web to the wrong side of [72] white background squares and [12] of each color of 4 1/2" squares.
3. Align the SEAM ALLOWANCE lines marked on the Creative Grids™ Circle Savvy Ruler with the bottom and left edges of a fused background square. Cut the arc using the 8" slot on the ruler to make a quarter-circle (Fig. 1). Repeat with the remaining fused white background squares and fused color squares.
4. Fuse a white background quarter-circle to [12] of each color of 4 1/2"square, aligning the bottom and left edges (Fig. 2). Stitch around the arc using the appliqué stitch of your choice. I recommend Edge Stitch, Blanket Stitch, Zig Zag Stitch, or Satin Stitch.
5. Repeat Step 4 to fuse a color quarter-circle to each of [72] 4 1/2" white background squares, aligning the bottom and left edges (Fig. 3). Stitch around the arc using the appliqué stitch of your choice.

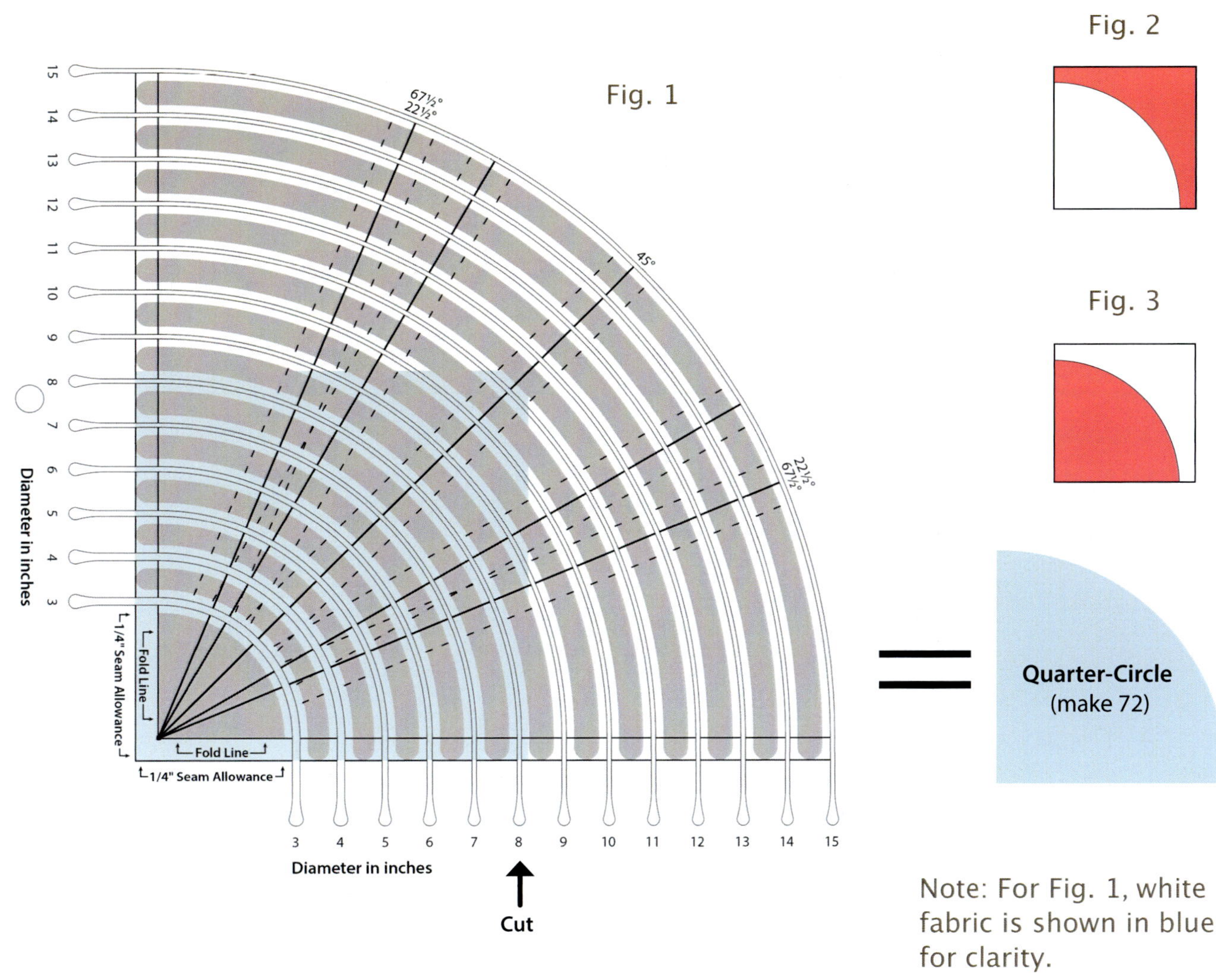

Note: For Fig. 1, white fabric is shown in blue for clarity.

QUILT TOP

ASSEMBLING THE QUILT TOP

Refer to Quilt Top for assembly.

1. Arrange all units and squares as shown. Sew blocks together into horizontal rows and press. Sew rows together and press to complete Quilt Top.

COMPLETING THE QUILT

1. Follow Quilting, page 60, to mark, layer, and quilt as desired. Quilt shown is quilted with a different pattern in each background and colored area.

2. Follow Making a Hanging Sleeve, page 64, if a hanging sleeve is desired.

3. Use binding strips and follow Making Straight-Grain Binding, page 65, to make binding. Follow Attaching Binding with Mitered Corners, page 66, to bind quilt.

QUARTER-CIRCLE

Option for Cutting Quarter-Circles:
Lay the template plastic on the quarter-circle pattern and trace. Cut template from plastic. Align the straight edges of the quarter-circle template with the bottom and left edges of the fused square. Cut along curved edge of template.

The Places You'll Go

The "The Places You'll Go" baby quilt is an adventurous addition to your little one's nursery. Made from soft turquoise and black flannel, it features playful designs of bears, arrows, and leaves that evoke exploration and discovery. The blocks are arranged to create large arrows, symbolizing the exciting journeys ahead. With its cozy textures, this quilt is perfect for both playtime and restful moments.

QUILT TOP CENTER

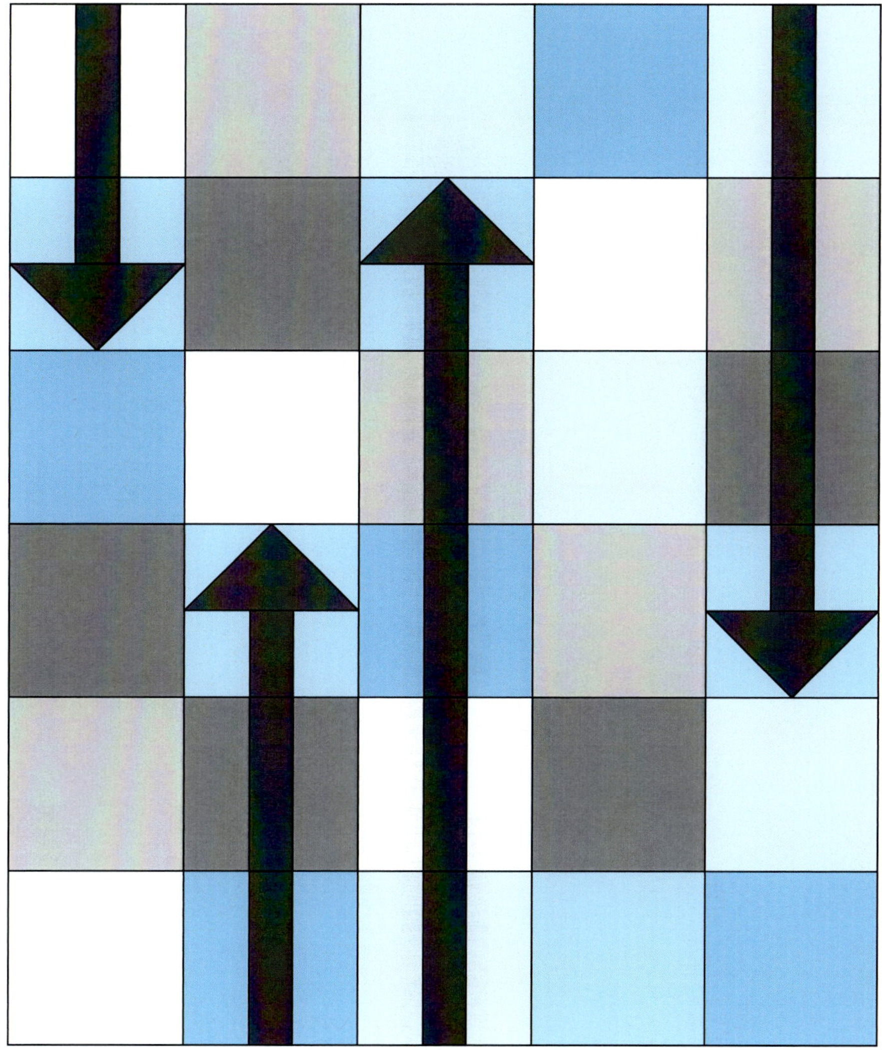

Design by Susan Emory

YARDAGE REQUIREMENTS

Yardage is based on 43"/44" wide fabric with a usable width of 40".

$^3/_8$ yds (34 cm) each of 5 print fabrics for backgrounds

$^1/_2$ yd (46 cm) of fabric for backgrounds of arrow points (blue solid)

$^1/_2$ yd (46 cm) of fabric for arrows (black print)

$^3/_4$ yd (39 cm) of fabric for border

$3^5/_8$ yds (3.3 m) of fabric for backing

$^1/_2$ yd (46 cm) of fabric for binding

You will also need:

56" x 64" (142 cm x 163 cm) piece of batting

FINISHED BLOCK SIZE:

8" x 8"
(20 cm x 20 cm)

FINISHED QUILT SIZE:

48" x 56"
(122 cm x 142 CM)

CUTTING THE PIECES

Follow Rotary Cutting, page 56, to cut fabric. WOF = cut strips across width of fabric from selvage to selvage. Border is cut exact length.

All measurements include $^1/_4$" seam allowances.

From each of 5 print fabrics for background:

- Cut [1] $8^1/_2$" x WOF strips; from this strip, cut [3] $8^1/_2$" squares.
- Cut [1] $3^1/_2$" x WOF strip; from this strip, cut [4] $3^1/_2$" x $8^1/_2$" rectangles.

From fabric for backgrounds of arrow points:

- Cut [1] $8^1/_2$" x WOF strip; from this strip, cut [1] $8^1/_2$" square.
- Cut remainder of strip into [2] $3^1/_2$" strips and from these strips, cut [8] $3^1/_2$" x $4^1/_2$" rectangles.
- Cut [1] $4^1/_2$" x WOF strip; from this strip, cut [8] $4^1/_2$" squares.

From fabric for arrows:

- Cut [1] $8^1/_2$" x WOF strip; from this strip, cut [10] $2^1/_2$" x $8^1/_2$" rectangles and [4] $2^1/_2$" x $4^1/_2$" rectangles.
- Cut [1] $4^1/_2$" x WOF strip; from this strip, cut [4] $4^1/_2$" x $8^1/_2$" rectangles.

From fabric for border:

- Cut [5] $4^1/_2$" x WOF strips.

From fabric for binding:

- Cut [6] $2^1/_2$" x WOF strips.

MAKING THE UNITS

Follow Machine Piecing and Pressing, page 57, to make quilt top. Use $^1/_4$" seam allowances throughout.

1. Draw a diagonal line on the wrong side of [8] $4^1/_2$" arrow point background squares. With right sides together, place a $4^1/_2$" background square on the corner of $4^1/_2$" x $8^1/_2$" arrow fabric rectangle (Fig. 1). Stitch diagonally on the drawn line (Fig. 2). Trim $^1/_4$" from stitching line (Fig. 3) and press toward background fabric (Fig. 4).

2. Add a second $4^1/_2$" arrow point background square to adjacent corner (Fig. 5), trim $^1/_4$" from stitching line (Fig. 6) and press toward background fabric to complete Flying Geese Unit. Repeat to make a total of 4 Flying Geese Units.

3. Arrange [1] $2^1/_2$" x $4^1/_2$" arrow fabric rectangle and [2] $3^1/_2$" x $4^1/_2$" arrow background rectangles as shown. Sew a background rectangle to each side of arrow rectangle. Press toward background fabric to complete the Background Unit. Repeat to make a total of 4 background units.

4. Sew a flying geese unit to each background unit and press toward background unit to complete Unit 1. Repeat to make a total of 4 Unit 1's.

5. Sew a matching $3^1/_2$" x $8^1/_2$" background rectangle to each side of a $2^1/_2$" x $8^1/_2$" arrow rectangle to make Unit 2. Press toward darker fabric. Repeat to make a total of 10 Unit 2's.

Fig. 1

Fig. 2

Fig. 3

Fig. 4

Fig. 5

Fig. 6

ASSEMBLING THE QUILT TOP

Refer to Quilt Top for assembly.

1. Sew units and squares together in horizontal rows. Press seam allowances in opposite directions in each row. Sew rows together to complete Quilt Top Center.

2. Trim selvages from [5] $4^1/_2$" x WOF border strips and sew together end to end. Cut [4] border strips $48^1/_2$" long. Sew a border strip to each side of quilt. Press toward border strips. Sew a border strip to top and bottom of quilt. Press toward border strips to complete Quilt Top.

COMPLETING THE QUILT

1. Follow Quilting, page 60, to mark, layer, and quilt as desired. Quilt shown is quilted with randomly spaced vertical lines.

2. Follow Making a Hanging Sleeve, page 64, if a hanging sleeve is desired.

3. Use binding strips and follow Making Straight-Grain Binding, page 65, to make binding. Follow Attaching Binding with Mitered Corners, page 66, to bind quilt.

Flying Geese Unit (make 4)

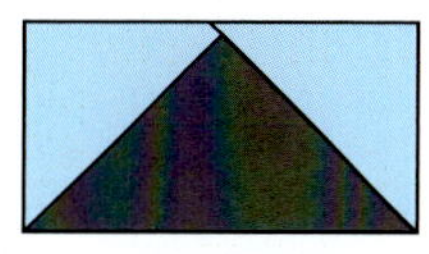

Background Unit (make 4)

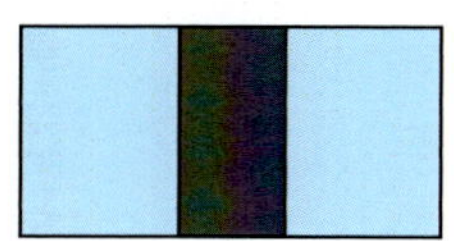

Unit 1 (make 4)

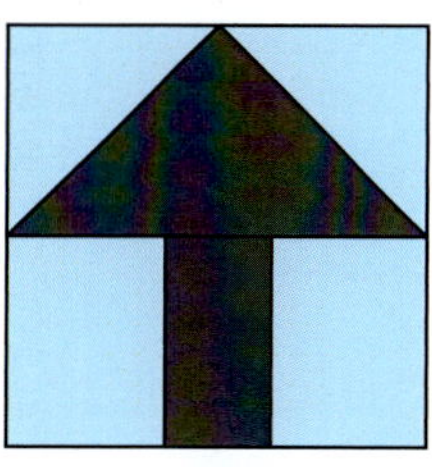

Unit 2 (make 10)

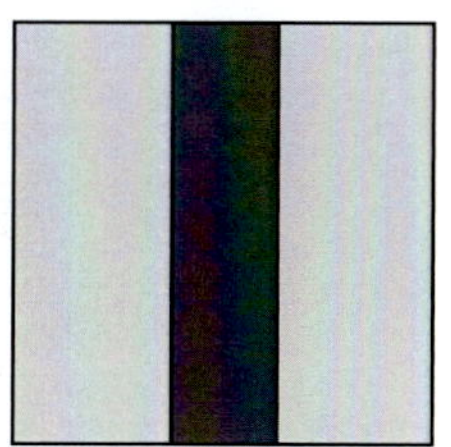

QUILT TOP

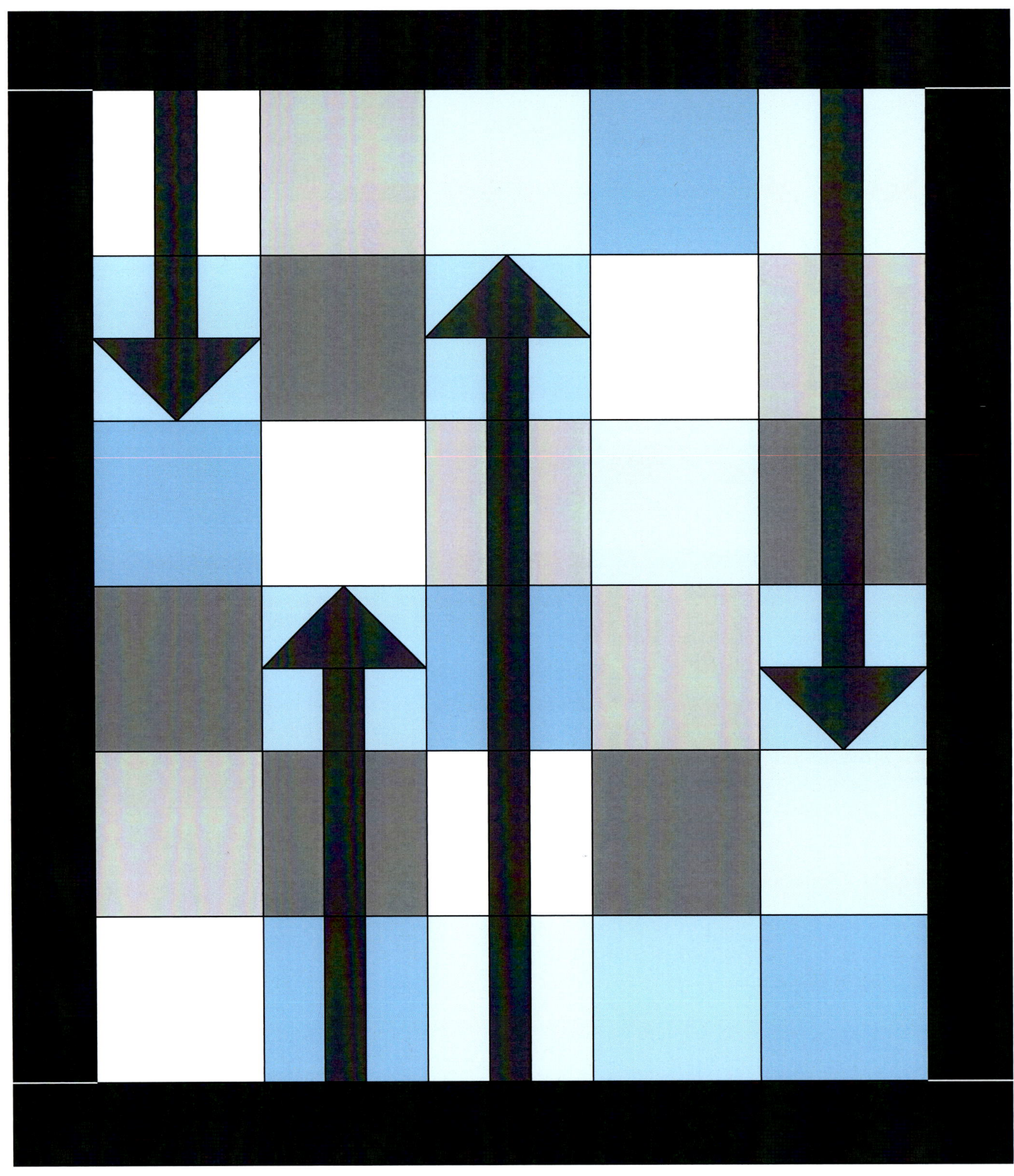

General Instructions

To make your quilting easier and more enjoyable, we encourage you to carefully read all of the general instructions, study the color photographs, and familiarize yourself with the individual project instructions before beginning a project.

FABRICS

SELECTING FABRICS

Choose high-quality, medium-weight 100% cotton fabrics. All-cotton fabrics hold a crease better, fray less, and are easier to quilt than cotton/polyester blends.

Yardage requirements listed for each project are based on 43"/44" wide fabric with a "usable" width of 40" after shrinkage and trimming selvages. Actual usable width will probably vary slightly from fabric to fabric. Our recommended yardage lengths should be adequate for occasional re-squaring of fabric when many cuts are required.

PREPARING FABRICS

We recommend that all fabrics be washed, dried, and pressed before cutting. If fabrics are not pre-washed, washing the finished quilt will cause shrinkage and give it a more "antiqued" look and feel. Bright and dark colors, which may run, should always be washed before cutting. After washing and drying fabric, fold lengthwise with wrong sides together and matching selvages.

ROTARY CUTTING

Rotary cutting has brought speed and accuracy to quiltmaking by allowing quilters to easily cut strips of fabric and then cut those strips into smaller pieces.

- Place fabric on work surface with fold closest to you.
- Cut all strips from the selvage-to-selvage width of the fabric unless otherwise indicated in project instructions.
- Square left edge of fabric using rotary cutter and rulers (Figs. 1 - 2).

Fig. 1

Fig. 2

- To cut each strip required for a project, place ruler over cut edge of fabric, aligning desired marking on ruler with cut edge; make cut (Fig. 3).

Fig. 3

- When cutting several strips from a single piece of fabric, it is important to make sure that cuts remain at a perfect right angle to the fold; square fabric as needed.

PIECING

Precise cutting, followed by accurate piecing, will ensure that all pieces of quilt top fit together well.

HAND PIECING

- Use ruler and sharp fabric marking pencil to draw all seam lines and transfer any alignment markings onto back of cut pieces.
- Matching right sides, pin two pieces together, using pins to mark corners.
- Use Running Stitch to sew pieces together along drawn line, backstitching at beginning and end of seam.
- Do not extend stitches into seam allowances.
- Run five or six stitches onto needle before pulling needle through fabric.
- To add stability, backstitch every 3/4" to 1".

MACHINE PIECING

- Set sewing machine stitch length for approximately 11 stitches per inch.
- Use neutral-colored general-purpose sewing thread (not quilting thread) in needle and in bobbin.
- An accurate 1/4" seam allowance is essential. Presser feet that are 1/4" wide are available for most sewing machines.
- When piecing, always place pieces right sides together and match raw edges; pin if necessary.
- Chain piecing saves time and will usually result in more accurate piecing.
- Trim away points of seam allowances that extend beyond edges of sewn pieces.

SEWING STRIP SETS

When there are several strips to assemble into a strip set, first sew strips together into pairs, then sew pairs together to form strip set. To help avoid distortion, sew seams in opposite directions (Fig. 4).

Fig. 4

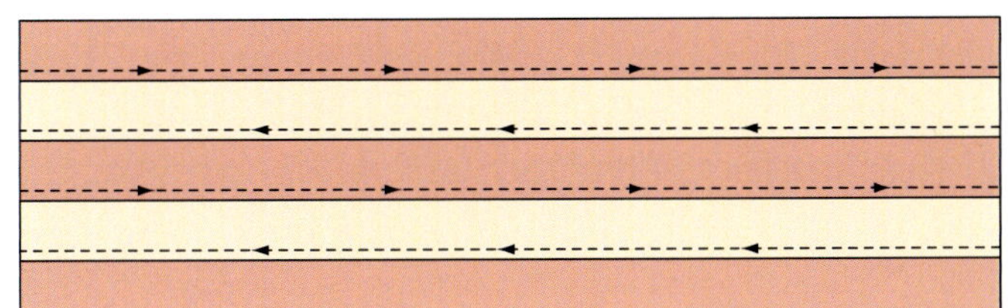

SEWING ACROSS SEAM INTERSECTIONS

When sewing across intersection of two seams, place pieces right sides together and match seams exactly, making sure seam allowances are pressed in opposite directions (Fig. 5).

Fig. 5

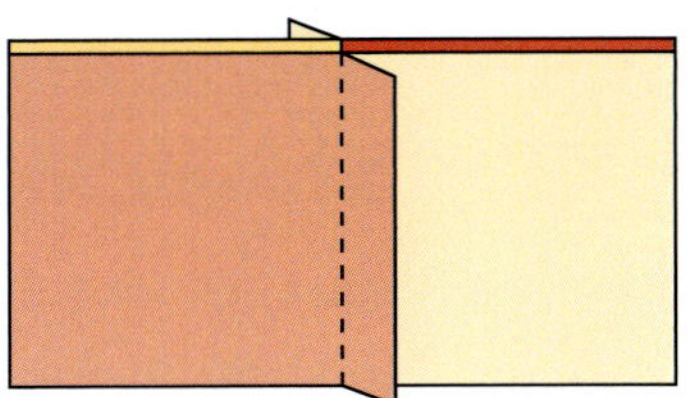

SEWING SHARP POINTS

To ensure sharp points when joining triangular or diagonal pieces, stitch across the center of the "X" (shown in pink) formed on wrong side by previous seams (Fig. 6).

Fig. 6

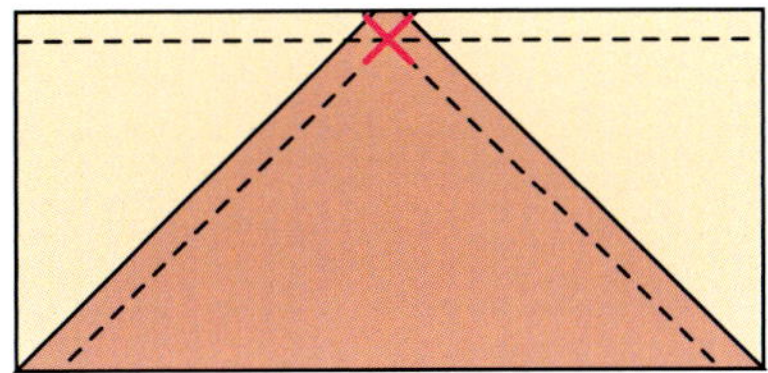

PRESSING

- Use steam iron set on "Cotton" for all pressing.
- Press after sewing each seam.
- Seam allowances are almost always pressed to one side, usually toward darker fabric. However, to reduce bulk it may occasionally be necessary to press seam allowances toward the lighter fabric or even to press them open.
- To prevent dark fabric seam allowance from showing through light fabric, trim darker seam allowance slightly narrower than lighter seam allowance.
- To press long seams, such as those in long strip sets, without curving or other distortion, lay strips across width of the ironing board.

MACHINE APPLIQUÉ

PREPARING FUSIBLE APPLIQUÉS

White or light-colored fabrics may need to be lined with fusible interfacing before applying fusible web to prevent darker fabrics from showing through.

1. Place paper-backed fusible web, paper side up, over appliqué pattern. Trace pattern onto paper side of web with pencil as many times as indicated in project instructions for a single fabric.
2. Follow manufacturer's instructions to fuse traced patterns to wrong side of fabrics. Do not remove paper backing. (Note: Some pieces may be given as measurements, such as a 2" x 4" rectangle, instead of drawn patterns. Fuse web to wrong side of fabrics indicated for these pieces.)
3. Use scissors to cut out appliqué pieces along traced lines; use rotary cutting equipment to cut out appliqué pieces given as measurements. Remove paper backing from all pieces.

MACHINE BLANKET STITCH APPLIQUÉ

Some sewing machines feature a Blanket Stitch. Refer to your owner's manual for machine set-up. If your machine does not have this stitch, try any of the decorative stitches your machine has until you are satisfied with the look.

1. Thread sewing machine and bobbin with 100% cotton thread in desired weight.
2. Attach open-toe presser foot. Select far right needle position and needle down (if your machine has these features).
3. If needed, pin commercial stabilizer to wrong side of background fabric or stabilize with spray starch.
4. Bring bobbin thread to the top of the fabric by lowering then raising the needle, bringing up the bobbin thread loop. Pull the loop all the way to the surface.
5. Begin by stitching 5 or 6 stitches in place (drop feed dogs or set stitch length at 0) or, use your machine's lock stitch feature, if equipped, to anchor thread. Return settings to selected decorative stitch.
6. Most of the Blanket Stitch should be done on the appliqué with the right edges of the stitch falling at the very outside edge of the appliqué. Stitch over all exposed raw edges of appliqué pieces.
7. (Note: Dots on Figs. 7-13 indicate where to leave needle in fabric when pivoting.) Always stopping with needle down in background fabric, refer to Fig. 7 to stitch outside points (like tips of leaves). Stop one stitch short of point. Raise presser foot. Pivot project slightly, lower presser foot, and make one angled Stitch 1. Take next stitch, stop at point, and pivot so Stitch 2 will be perpendicular to point. Pivot slightly to make Stitch 3. Continue stitching.

Fig. 7

8. For outside corners (Figs. 8-9), stitch to the corner, stopping with the needle in the background fabric. Raise presser foot. Pivot project, lower presser foot, and take an angled stitch. Raise presser foot. Pivot project, lower presser foot and stitch adjacent side.

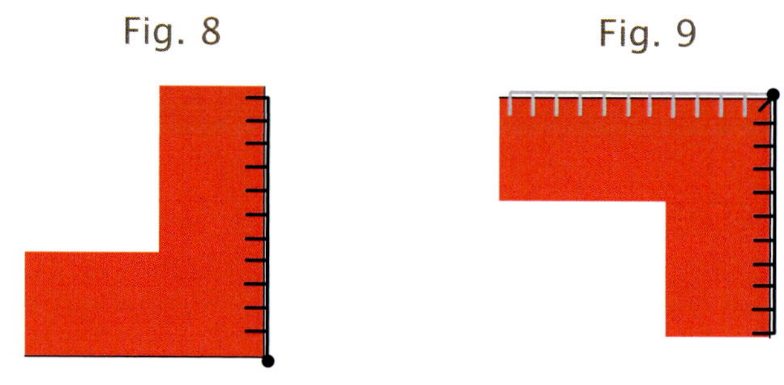
Fig. 8 Fig. 9

9. For inside corners (Fig. 10-11), stitch to the corner, taking the last bite at corner and stopping with the needle down in background fabric. Raise presser foot. Pivot project, lower presser foot, and take an angled stitch. Raise presser foot. Pivot project, lower presser foot, and stitch adjacent side.

Fig. 10

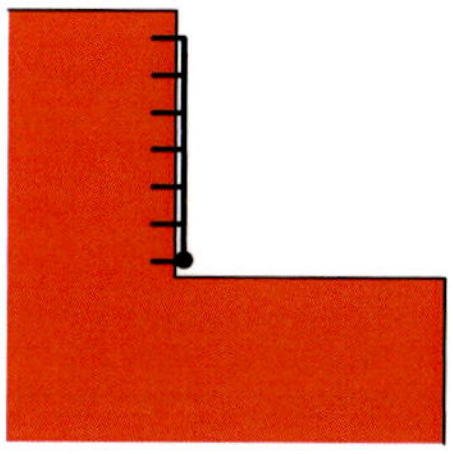

Fig. 11

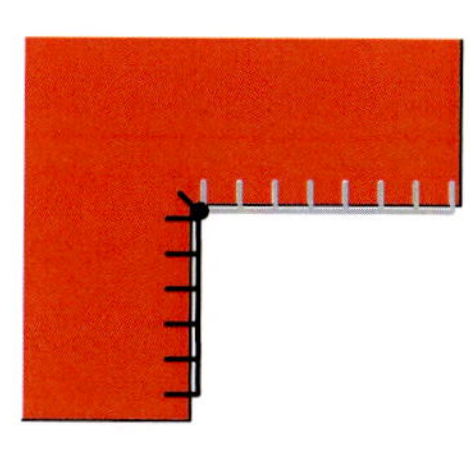

10. When stitching outside curves (Fig. 12), stop with needle down in background fabric. Raise presser foot and pivot project as needed. Lower presser foot and continue stitching, pivoting as often as necessary to follow curve. Small circles may require pivoting between each stitch.

Fig. 12

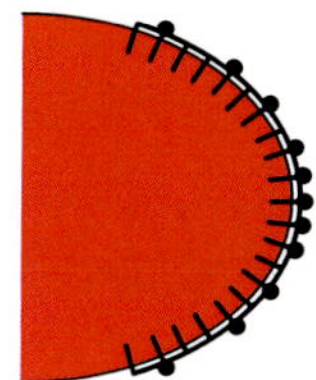

11. When stitching inside curves (Fig. 13), stop with needle down in background fabric. Raise presser foot and pivot project as needed. Lower presser foot and continue stitching, pivoting as often as necessary to follow curve.

Fig. 13

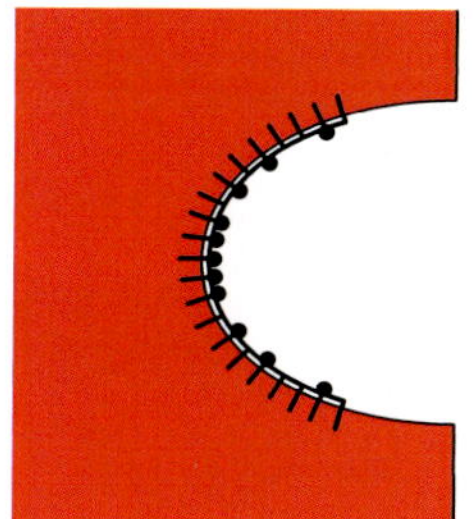

12. When ending stitching, use a lock stitch to sew 5 or 6 stitches in place or use a needle to pull threads to wrong side of background fabric (Fig. 14); knot then trim ends.

Fig. 14

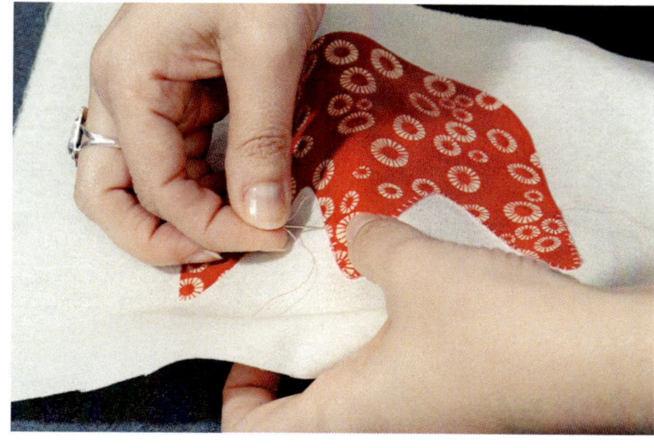

13. Carefully tear away stabilizer, if used.

BORDERS

Borders cut along the lengthwise grain will lay flatter and smoother than borders cut along the crosswise grain. Lengthwise-grain borders are especially important for bed-size quilts, since the more stable lengthwise grain is less likely to stretch out of shape and cause wavy edges. Our instructions for cutting borders for bed-size quilts also include an extra 2" at each end for "insurance"; borders will be trimmed after measuring completed center section of quilt top. And, as always, you should match right sides and raw edges and use a $^{1}/_{4}$" seam allowance when sewing.

ADDING SQUARED BORDERS

1. Mark the center of each edge of quilt top.
2. Squared borders are usually added to top and bottom, then side edges, of the center section of a quilt top. To add top border, measure across center of quilt top to determine length of border (Fig. 15). Trim border to the determined length.

Fig. 15

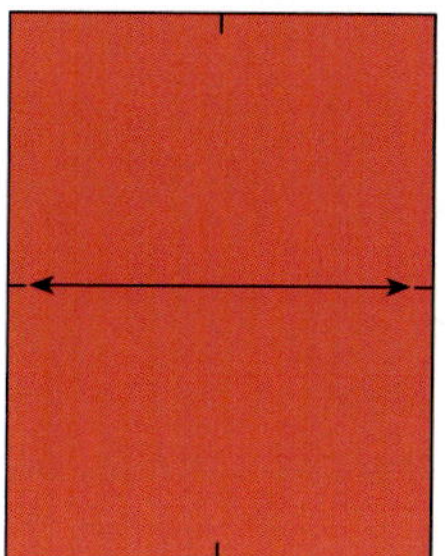

3. Mark center of 1 long edge of border. Matching center marks and raw edges, pin border to quilt top, easing in any fullness; stitch.
4. Repeat Steps 2 and 3 to add bottom border to quilt top.
5. Measure center of quilt top (including attached borders) to determine length of side borders. Repeat Steps 2 and 3 to add side borders to quilt top (Fig. 16).

Fig. 16

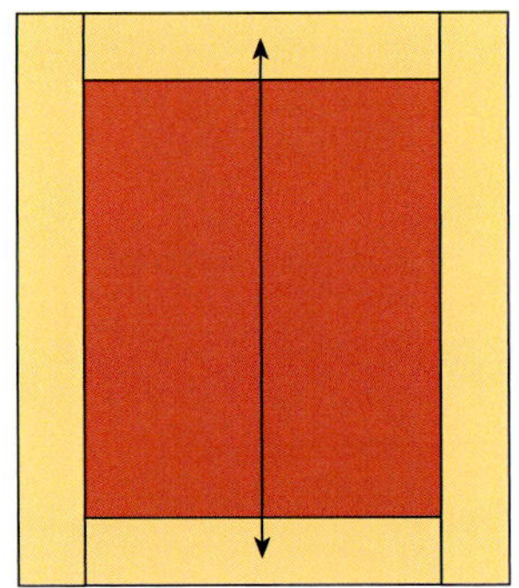

ADDING MITERED BORDERS

1. Mark the center of each edge of quilt top (see Fig. 15).
2. Mark center of 1 long edge of top border. Measure across center of quilt top (see Fig. 15). Matching center marks and raw edges, pin border to center of quilt top edge. From center of border, measure out $^{1}/_{2}$ the width of the quilt top in both directions and mark. Match marks on border with corners of quilt top and pin. Easing in any fullness, pin border to quilt top between center and corners. Sew border to quilt top, beginning and ending seams exactly $^{1}/_{4}$" from each corner of quilt top and backstitching at beginning and end of stitching (Fig. 17).

Fig. 17

3. Repeat Step 2 to sew bottom, then side borders, to center section of quilt top. To temporarily move first 2 borders out of the way, fold and pin ends as shown in Fig. 18.

Fig. 18

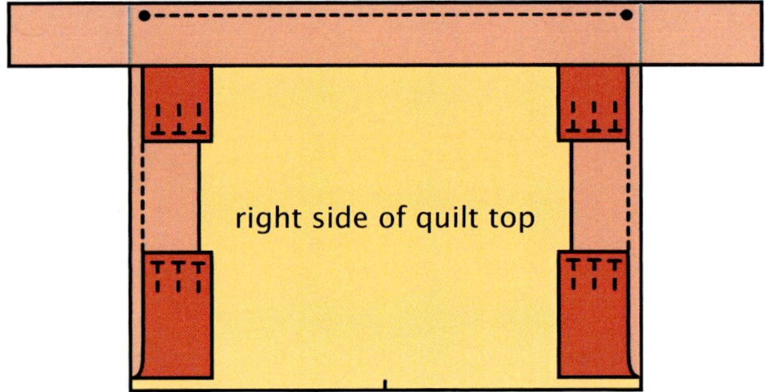

4. Fold 1 corner of quilt top diagonally with right sides together; use rotary cutting ruler to mark stitching line as shown in Fig.19. Pin strips together along drawn line. Sew on drawn line, backstitching at beginning and end of stitching (Fig. 20).

Fig. 19 Fig. 20

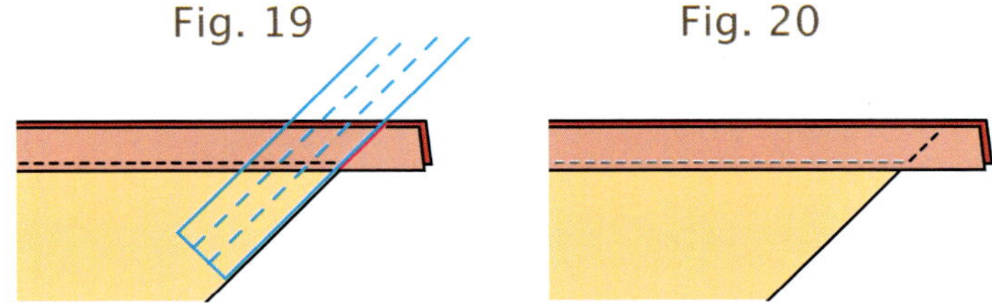

5. Turn mitered corner right side up. Check to see that there is not a gap at the inner end of the seam and that corner does not pucker.
6. Trim seam allowances to $^{1}/_{4}$"; press to 1 side.
7. Repeat Steps 4-6 to miter each remaining corner.

QUILTING

Quilting holds the three layers (top, batting, and backing) of the quilt together and can be done by hand or machine. Because marking, layering, and quilting are interrelated and may be done in different orders depending on circumstances, please read entire Quilting section, pages 60 – 64, before beginning project.

TYPES OF QUILTING DESIGNS

IN THE DITCH QUILTING

Quilting along seamlines or along edges of appliquéd pieces is called "in the ditch" quilting. This type of quilting should be done on side opposite seam allowance and does not have to be marked.

OUTLINE QUILTING

Quilting a consistent distance, usually $^{1}/_{4}$", from seam or appliqué is called "outline" quilting. Outline quilting may be marked, or $^{1}/_{4}$" masking tape may be placed along seamlines for quilting guide. (Do not leave tape on quilt longer than necessary, since it may leave an adhesive residue.)

MOTIF QUILTING

Quilting a design, such as a feathered wreath, is called "motif" quilting. This type of quilting should be marked before basting quilt layers together.

ECHO QUILTING

Quilting that follows the outline of an appliquéd or pieced design with two or more parallel lines is called "echo" quilting. This type of quilting does not need to be marked.

CHANNEL QUILTING

Quilting with straight, parallel lines is called "channel" quilting. This type of quilting may be marked or stitched using a guide.

CROSSHATCH QUILTING

Quilting straight lines in a grid pattern is called "crosshatch" quilting. Lines may be stitched parallel to edges of quilt or stitched diagonally. This type of quilting may be marked or stitched using a guide.

MEANDERING QUILTING

Quilting in random curved lines and swirls is called "meandering" quilting. Quilting lines should not cross or touch each other. This type of quilting does not need to be marked.

STIPPLE QUILTING

Meandering quilting that is very closely spaced is called "stipple" quilting. Stippling will flatten the area quilted and is often stitched in background areas to raise appliquéd or pieced designs. This type of quilting does not need to be marked.

MARKING QUILTING LINES

Quilting lines may be marked using fabric marking pencils, chalk markers, water- or air-soluble pens, or lead pencils. Simple quilting designs may be marked with chalk or chalk pencil after basting. A small area may be marked, then quilted, before moving to next area to be marked. Intricate designs should be marked before basting using a more durable marker.

Caution: Pressing may permanently set some marks. Test different markers on scrap fabric to find one that marks clearly and can be thoroughly removed.

A wide variety of pre-cut quilting stencils, as well as entire books of quilting patterns, are available. Using a stencil makes it easier to mark intricate or repetitive designs.

To make a stencil from a pattern, center template plastic over pattern and use a permanent marker to trace pattern onto plastic. Use a craft knife with single or double blade to cut channels along traced lines (Fig. 21).

Fig. 21

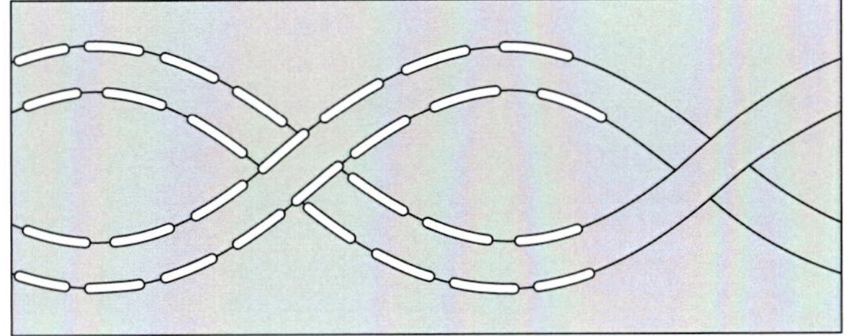

PREPARING THE BACKING

To allow for slight shifting of quilt top during quilting, backing should be approximately 4" larger on all sides. Yardage requirements listed for quilt backings are calculated for 43"/44"w fabric. Using 90"w or 108"w fabric for the backing of a bed-sized quilt may eliminate piecing. To piece a backing using 43"/44"w fabric, use the following instructions.

1. Measure length and width of quilt top; add 8" to each measurement.
2. If determined width is 79" or less, cut backing fabric into two lengths slightly longer than determined length measurement. Trim selvages. Place lengths with right sides facing and sew long edges together, forming tube (Fig. 22). Match seams and press along one fold (Fig. 23). Cut along pressed fold to form single piece (Fig. 24).

Fig. 22

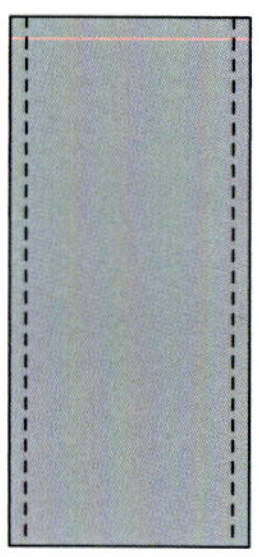

Fig. 23

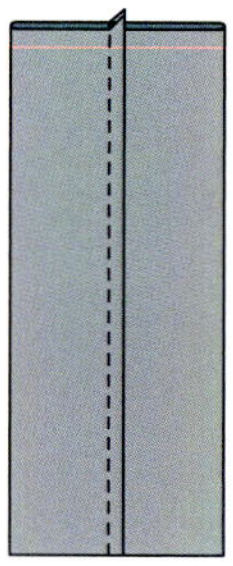

Fig. 24

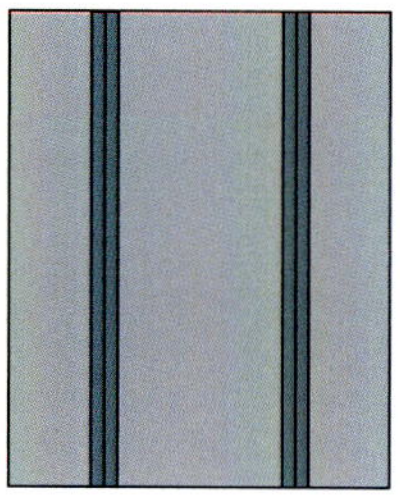

3. If determined width is more than 79", it may require less fabric yardage if the backing is pieced horizontally. Divide determined length measurement by 40" to determine how many widths will be needed. Cut required number of widths the determined width measurement. Trim selvages. Sew long edges together to form single piece.
4. Trim backing to size determined in Step 1; press seam allowances open.

CHOOSING THE BATTING

The appropriate batting will make quilting easier. For fine hand quilting, choose low-loft batting. All cotton or cotton/polyester blend battings work well for machine quilting because the cotton helps "grip" quilt layers. If quilt is to be tied, a high-loft batting, sometimes called extra-loft or fat batting, may be used to make quilt "fluffy."

Types of batting include cotton, polyester, wool, cotton/polyester blend, cotton/wool blend, and silk. When selecting batting, refer to package labels for characteristics and care instructions. Cut batting same size as prepared backing.

ASSEMBLING THE QUILT

1. Examine wrong side of quilt top closely; trim any seam allowances and clip any threads that may show through front of the quilt. Press quilt top, being careful not to "set" any marked quilting lines.
2. Place backing wrong side up on flat surface. Use masking tape to tape edges of backing to surface. Place batting on top of backing fabric. Smooth batting gently, being careful not to stretch or tear. Center quilt top right side up on batting.
3. If hand quilting, begin in center and work toward outer edges to hand baste all layers together. Use long stitches and place basting lines approximately 4" apart (Fig. 25). Smooth fullness or wrinkles toward outer edges.

Fig. 25

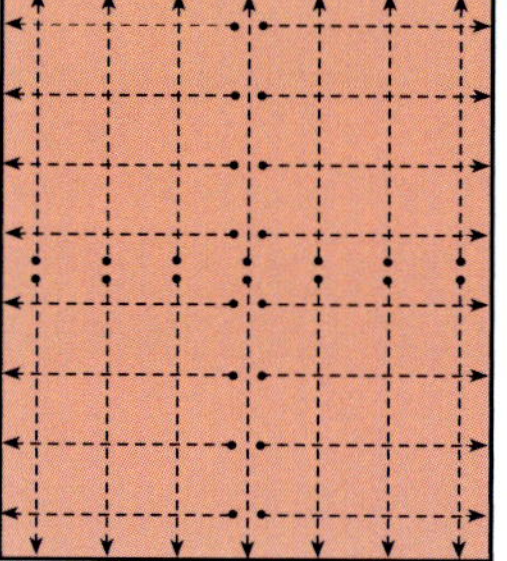

4. If machine quilting, use 1" rustproof safety pins to "pin-baste" all layers together, spacing pins approximately 4" apart. Begin at center and work toward outer edges to secure all layers. If possible, place pins away from areas that will be quilted, although pins may be removed as needed when quilting.

HAND QUILTING

The quilting stitch is a basic running stitch that forms a broken line on quilt top and backing. Stitches on quilt top and backing should be straight and equal in length.

1. Secure center of quilt in hoop or frame. Check quilt top and backing to make sure they are smooth. To help prevent puckers, always begin quilting in the center of quilt and work toward outside edges.
2. Thread needle with 18" - 20" length of quilting thread; knot one end. Using thimble, insert needle into quilt top and batting approximately 1/2" from quilting line. Bring needle up on quilting line (Fig. 26); when knot catches on quilt top, give thread a quick, short pull to "pop" knot through fabric into batting (Fig. 27).

Fig. 26

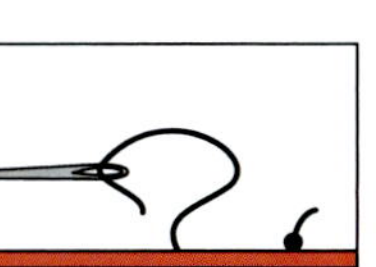

Fig. 27

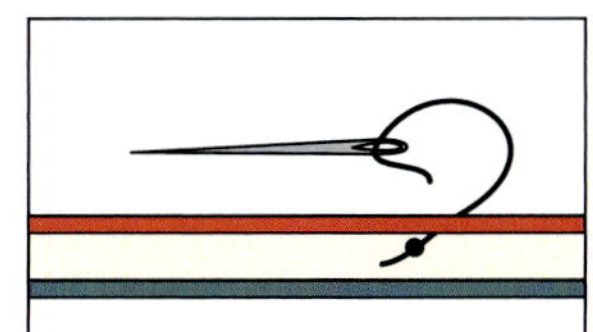

3. Holding needle with sewing hand and placing other hand underneath quilt, use thimble to push tip of needle down through all layers. As soon as needle touches finger underneath, use that finger to push tip of needle only back up through layers to top of quilt. (The amount of needle showing above fabric determines length of quilting stitch.) Referring to Fig. 28, rock needle up and down, taking three to six stitches before bringing needle and thread completely through layers. Check back of quilt to make sure stitches are going through all layers. If necessary, make one stitch at a time when quilting through seam allowances or along curves and corners.

Fig. 28

4. At end of thread, knot thread close to fabric and "pop" knot into batting; clip thread close to fabric.
5. Move hoop as often as necessary. Thread may be left dangling and picked up again after returning to that part of quilt.

MACHINE QUILTING METHODS

Use general-purpose thread in bobbin. Do not use quilting thread. Thread the needle of machine with general-purpose thread or transparent monofilament thread to make quilting blend with quilt top fabrics. Use decorative thread, such as a metallic or contrasting-color general-purpose thread, to make quilting lines stand out more.

STRAIGHT-LINE QUILTING

The term "straight-line" is somewhat deceptive, since curves (especially gentle ones) as well as straight lines can be stitched with this technique.

1. Set stitch length for six to ten stitches per inch and attach walking foot to sewing machine.
2. Determine which section of quilt will have longest continuous quilting line, oftentimes area from center top to center bottom. Roll up and secure each edge of quilt to help reduce the bulk, keeping fabrics smooth. Smaller projects may not need to be rolled.
3. Begin stitching on longest quilting line, using very short stitches for the first 1/4" to "lock" quilting. Stitch across project, using one hand on each side of walking foot to slightly spread fabric and to guide fabric through machine. Lock stitches at end of quilting line.
4. Continue machine quilting, stitching longer quilting lines first to stabilize quilt before moving on to other areas.

FREE-MOTION QUILTING

Free-motion quilting may be free form or may follow a marked pattern.

1. Attach darning foot to sewing machine and lower or cover feed dogs.
2. Position quilt under darning foot; lower foot. Holding top thread, take a stitch and pull bobbin thread to top of quilt. To "lock" beginning of quilting line, hold top and bobbin threads while making three to five stitches in place.
3. Use one hand on each side of darning foot to slightly spread fabric and to move fabric through the machine. Even stitch length is achieved by using smooth, flowing hand motion and steady machine speed. Slow machine speed and fast hand movement will create long stitches. Fast machine speed and slow hand movement will create short stitches. Move quilt sideways, back and forth, in a circular motion, or in a random motion to create desired designs; do not rotate quilt. Lock stitches at end of each quilting line.

TYING A QUILT

Tied quilts use yarn or floss ties instead of quilting stitches to secure the layers. For a tied quilt, be sure to use bonded batting to prevent separation or bunching when the quilt is laundered. You may also use a higher loft batting than when quilting.

1. Determine where ties will be placed and mark if necessary. Space ties evenly. On a pieced top, tie at corners of blocks or pieces within blocks.
2. Follow Preparing The Backing, page 62, and Assembling the Quilt, page 62, to prepare quilt for tying.
3. Thread a large darning needle with a long length of embroidery floss, yarn, or pearl cotton; do not knot.
4. At each mark or tie location, take a small stitch through all layers of quilt. Pull up floss, but do not cut between stitches (Fig. 29). Begin at center of quilt and work toward outside edges, rethreading needle as necessary.

Fig. 29

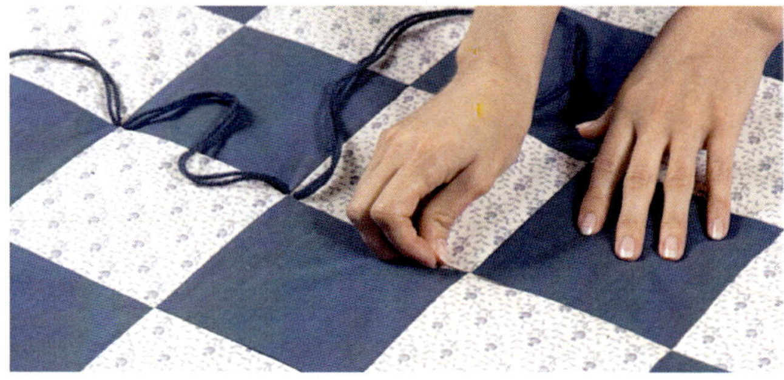

5. Cut floss between stitches. At each stitch, use a square knot to tie floss securely (Fig. 30); trim ties to desired length.

Fig. 30

MAKING A HANGING SLEEVE

Attaching a hanging sleeve to back of wall hanging or quilt before the binding is added allows project to be displayed on wall.

1. Measure width of quilt top edge and subtract 1". Cut piece of fabric 7"w by determined measurement.
2. Press short edges of fabric piece 1/4" to wrong side; press edges 1/4" to wrong side again and machine stitch in place.
3. Matching wrong sides, fold piece in half lengthwise to form tube.
4. Follow project instructions to sew binding to quilt top and to trim backing and batting. Before Blindstitching binding to backing, match raw edges and stitch hanging sleeve to center top edge on back of quilt.
5. Finish binding quilt, treating hanging sleeve as part of backing.
6. Blindstitch bottom of hanging sleeve to backing, taking care not to stitch through to front of quilt.

BINDING

Binding encloses the raw edges of quilt. Because of its stretchiness, bias binding works well for binding projects with curves or rounded corners and tends to lie smooth and flat in any given circumstance. Binding may also be cut from straight lengthwise or crosswise grain of fabric.

MAKING CONTINUOUS BIAS STRIP BINDING

Bias strips for binding can simply be cut and pieced to desired length. However, when a long length of binding is needed, the "continuous" method is quick and accurate.

1. Cut square from binding fabric the size indicated in project instructions. Cut square in half diagonally to make two triangles.
2. With right sides together and using $^1/_4$" seam allowance, sew triangles together (Fig. 31); press seam allowances open.

Fig. 31

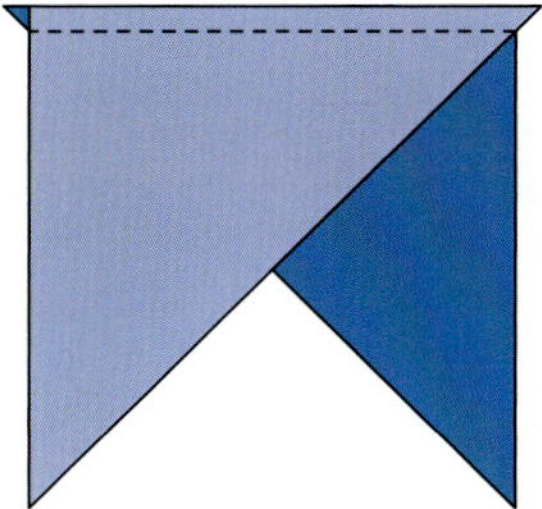

3. On wrong side of fabric, draw lines the width of binding as specified in project instructions, usually $2^1/_2$" (Fig. 32). Cut off any remaining fabric less than this width.

Fig. 32

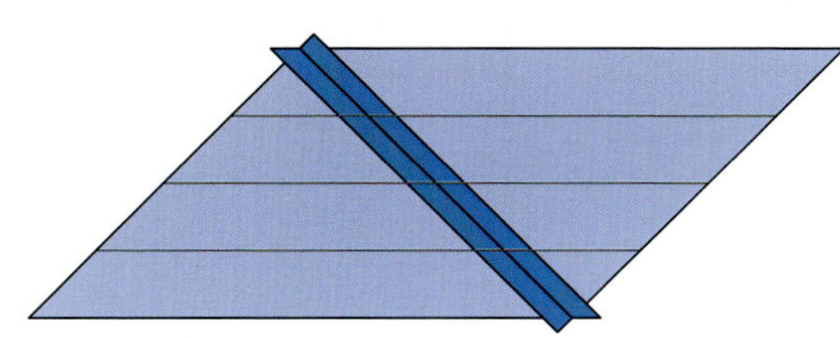

4. With right sides inside, bring short edges together to form tube; match raw edges so that first drawn line of top section meets second drawn line of bottom section (Fig. 33).

Fig. 33

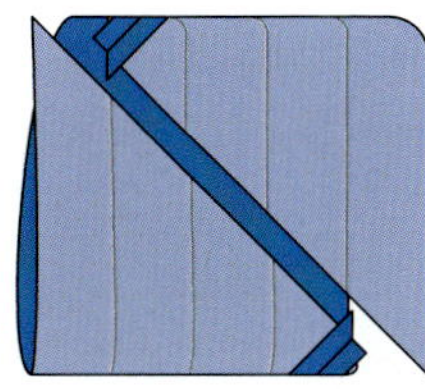

5. Carefully pin edges together by inserting pins through drawn lines at point where drawn lines intersect, making sure pins go through intersections on both sides. Using $^1/_4$" seam allowance, sew edges together; press seam allowances open.
6. To cut continuous strip, begin cutting along first drawn line (Fig. 34). Continue cutting along drawn line around tube.

Fig. 34

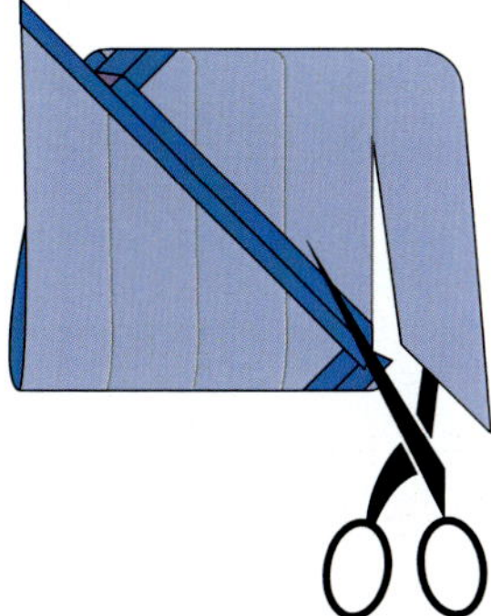

7. Trim ends of bias strip square.
8. Matching wrong sides and raw edges, carefully press bias strip in half lengthwise to complete binding.

MAKING STRAIGHT-GRAIN BINDING

1. To determine length of strip needed if attaching binding with mitered corners, measure edges of quilt and add 12".
2. To determine lengths of strips needed if attaching binding with overlapped corners, measure each edge of quilt; add 3" to each measurement.
3. Cut lengthwise or crosswise strips of binding fabric the determined length and the width called for in project instructions. Strips may be pieced using diagonal seams to achieve necessary length.
4. Matching wrong sides and raw edges, press strip(s) in half lengthwise to complete binding.

ATTACHING BINDING WITH MITERED CORNERS

1. Beginning with one end near center on bottom edge of quilt, lay binding around quilt to make sure that seams in binding will not end up at a corner. Adjust placement if necessary. Matching raw edges of binding to raw edge of quilt top, pin binding to right side of quilt along one edge.
2. When you reach first corner, mark 1/4" from corner of quilt top (Fig. 35).

Fig. 35

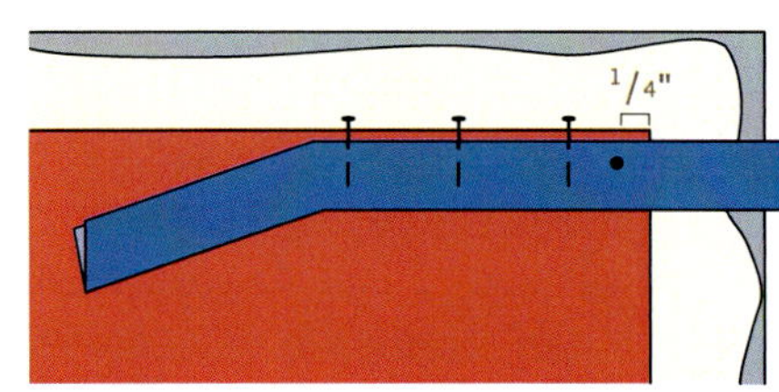

3. Beginning approximately 10" from end of binding and using 1/4" seam allowance, sew binding to quilt, backstitching at beginning of stitching and at mark (Fig. 36). Lift needle out of fabric and clip thread.

Fig. 36

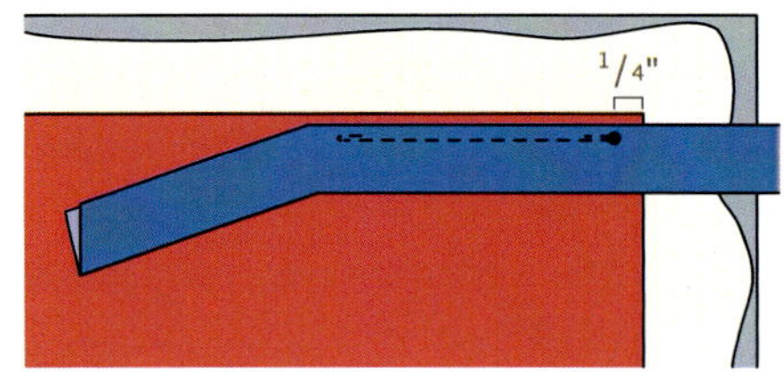

4. Fold binding as shown in Figs. 37 - 38 and pin binding to adjacent side, matching raw edges. When you've reached the next corner, mark 1/4" from edge of quilt top.

Fig. 37

Fig. 38

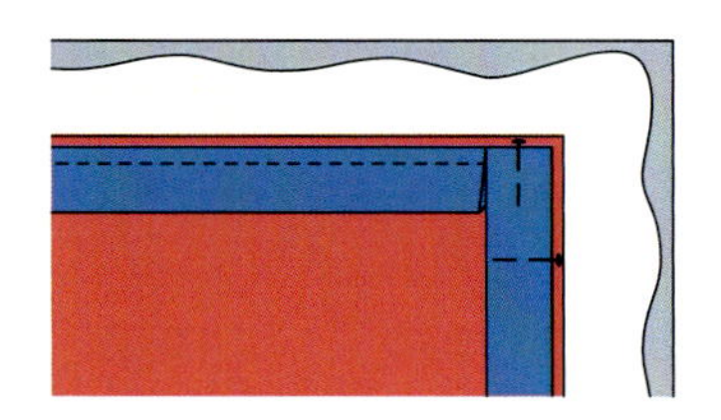

5. Backstitching at edge of quilt top, sew pinned binding to quilt (Fig. 39); backstitch at the next mark. Lift needle out of fabric and clip thread.

Fig. 39

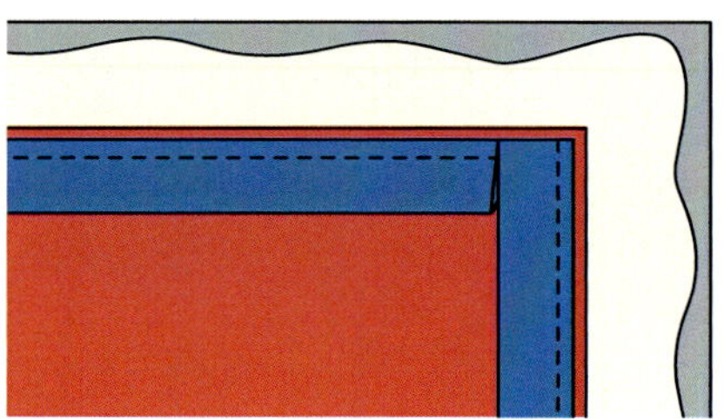

6. Continue sewing binding to quilt, stopping approximately 10" from starting point (Fig. 40).

Fig. 40

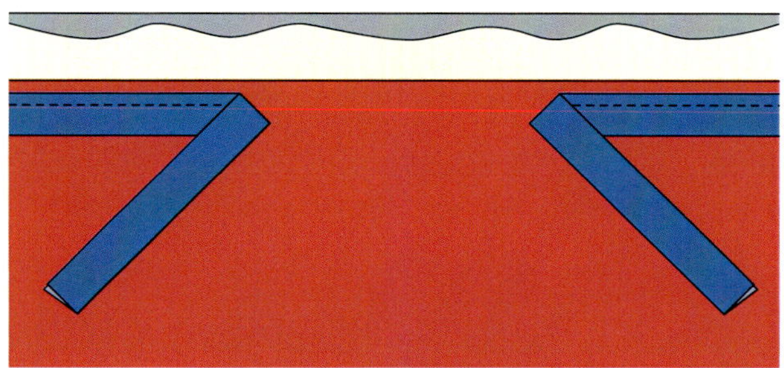

7. Bring beginning and end of binding to center of opening and fold each end back, leaving a 1/4" space between folds (Fig. 41). Finger press folds.

Fig. 41

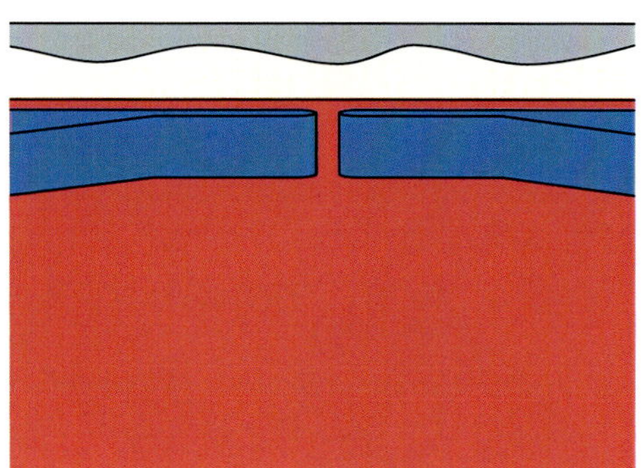

8. Unfold ends of binding and draw a line across wrong side in finger-pressed crease. Draw a line through the lengthwise pressed fold of binding at the same spot to create a cross mark. With edge of ruler at cross mark, line up 45° angle marking on ruler with one long side of binding. Draw a diagonal line from edge to edge. Repeat on remaining end, making sure that the two diagonal lines are angled the same way (Fig. 42).

Fig. 42

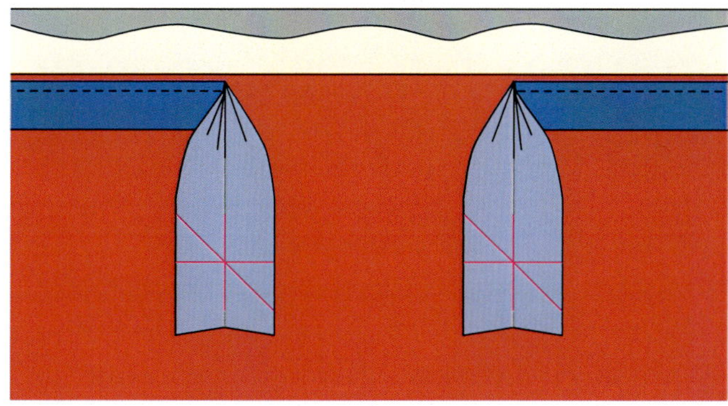

9. Matching right sides and diagonal lines, pin binding ends together at right angles (Fig. 43).

Fig. 43

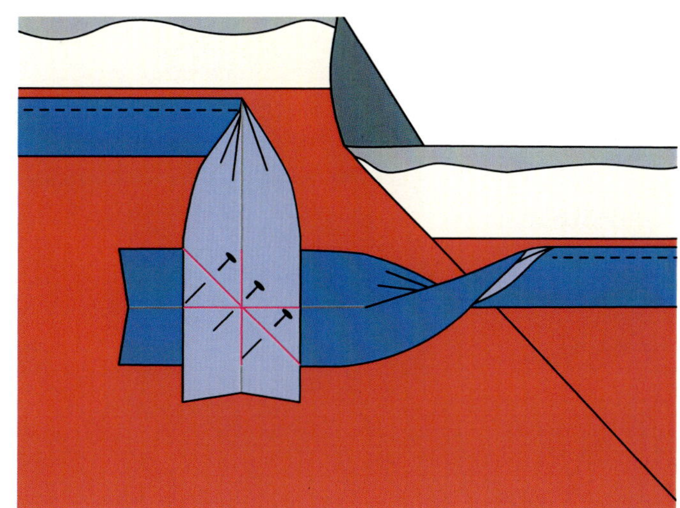

10. Machine stitch along diagonal line (Fig. 44), removing pins as you stitch.

Fig. 44

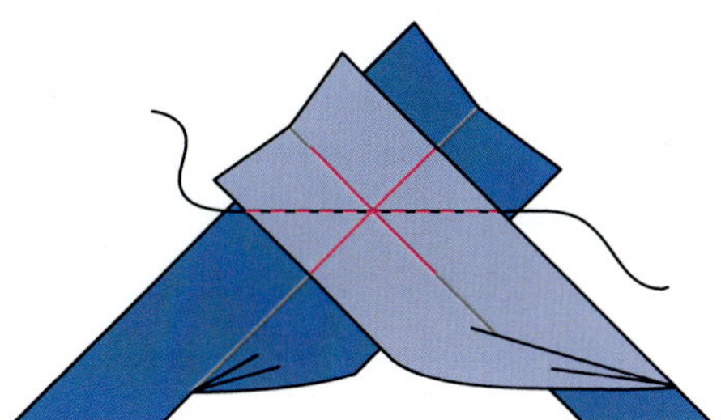

11. Lay binding against quilt to double check that it is correct length.
12. Trim binding ends, leaving 1/4" seam allowance; press seam open. Stitch binding to quilt.
13. Trim backing and batting a scant 1/4" larger than quilt top so that batting and backing will fill the binding when it is folded over to quilt backing.
14. On one edge of quilt, fold binding over to quilt backing and pin pressed edge in place, covering stitching line (Fig. 45). On adjacent side, fold binding over, forming a mitered corner (Fig. 46). Repeat to pin remainder of binding in place.

Fig. 45

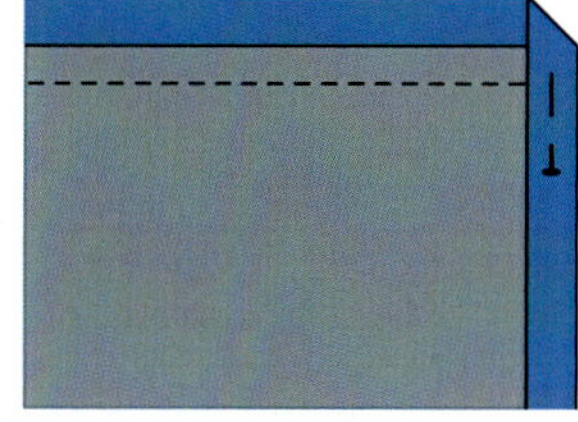

Fig. 46

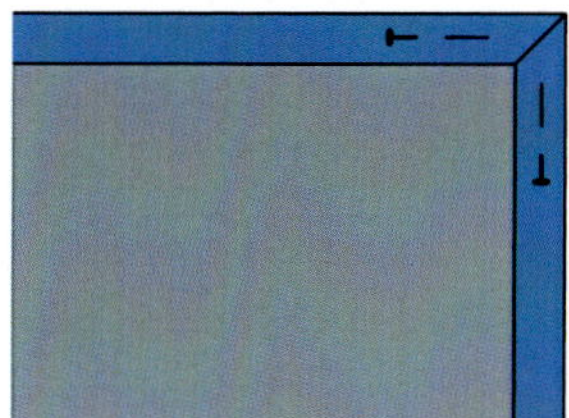

15. Blindstitch binding to backing, taking care not to stitch through to front of quilt.

ATTACHING BINDING WITH OVERLAPPED CORNERS

1. Matching raw edges and using $^1/_4$" seam allowance, sew a length of binding to top and bottom edges on right side of quilt.
2. Trim backing and batting a scant $^1/_4$" larger than quilt top so that batting and backing will fill the binding when it is folded over to quilt backing.
3. Trim ends of top and bottom binding even with edges of quilt top. Fold binding over to quilt backing and pin pressed edges in place, covering stitching line (Fig. 47); blindstitch binding to backing

Fig. 47

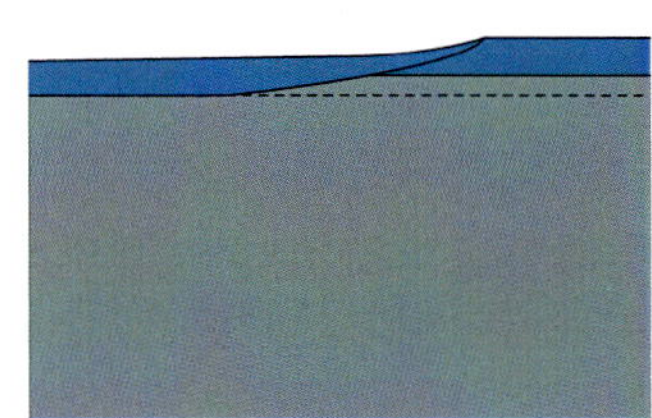

4. Leaving approximately $1^1/_2$" of binding at each end, stitch a length of binding to each side edge of quilt. Trim backing and batting as in Step 2.
5. Trim each end of binding $^1/_2$" longer than bound edge. Fold each end of binding over to quilt backing (Fig. 48); pin in place. Fold binding over to quilt backing and blindstitch in place, taking care not to stitch through to front of quilt.

Fig. 48

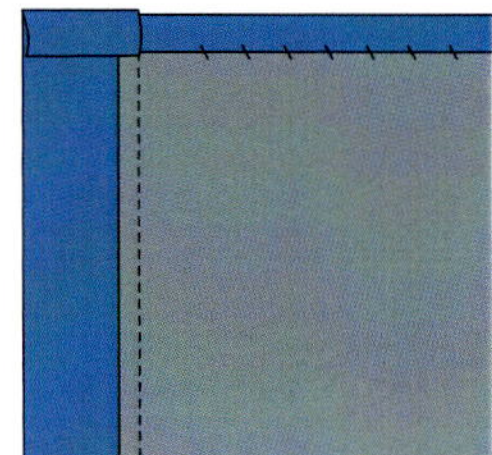

BLIND STITCH

Come up at 1, go down at 2, and come up at 3 (Fig. 49). Length of stitches may be varied as desired.

Fig. 49

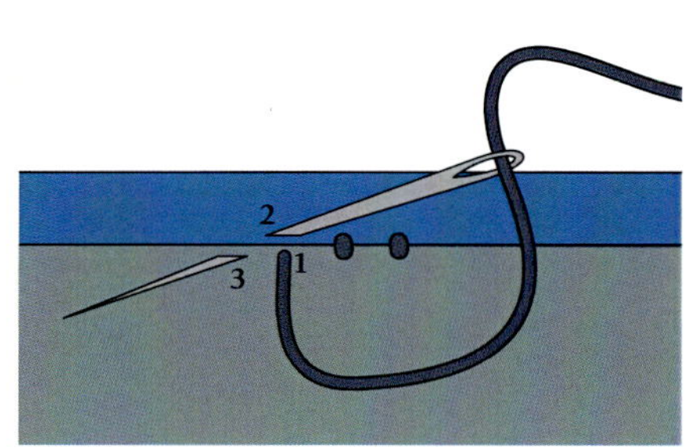

SIGNING AND DATING YOUR QUILT

A completed quilt is a work of art and should be signed and dated. There are many different ways to do this and numerous books on the subject. The label should reflect the style of the quilt, the occasion or person for which it was made, and the quilter's own particular talents. Following are suggestions for recording the history of quilt or adding a sentiment for future generations.

- Embroider quilter's name, date, and any additional information on quilt top or backing. Matching floss, such as cream floss on white border, will leave a subtle record. Bright or contrasting floss will make the information stand out.
- Make label from muslin and use permanent marker to write information. Use different colored permanent markers to make label more decorative. Stitch label to back of quilt.
- Use photo-transfer paper to add image to white or cream fabric label. Stitch label to back of quilt.
- Piece an extra block from quilt top pattern to use as label. Add information with permanent fabric pen. Appliqué block to back of quilt.
- Write message on appliquéd design from quilt top. Attach appliqué to back of the quilt.

Made in U.S.A.